# *WRITE YOUR OWN WEDDING*

# WRITE YOUR OWN WEDDING

## Revised and Updated

### Mordecai L. Brill
### Marlene Halpin
### William H. Genné

NEW CENTURY PUBLISHERS, INC.

The poem "Love" by Roy Croft is from *The Best Loved Poems of the American People* selected by Hazel Felleman. Published by Doubleday & Company, Inc., 1936. Used by permission.

Excerpts from the English translation of the Rite of Marriage © 1969, International Committee on English in the Liturgy, Inc. All rights reserved.

**Library of Congress Cataloging in Publication Data**

Brill, Mordecai L.
    Write your own wedding.

    Includes bibliographical references.
    1. Marriage service.    2. Weddings.    I. Halpin, Marlene
II. Genné, William H.   III. Title.
BL619.M37B75  1985      291.3'8     85–7156
ISBN 0–8329–0398–1

To those people who, in their search for honesty and integrity, are thinking through the meaning of their wedding ceremony to their marriage.

God creates new worlds
each day by causing
marriages to take place.

from *The Zohar*
a 14th-century collection of
teachings on Jewish mysticism

# CONTENTS

*Write Your Own Wedding*

# *A PERSONAL NOTE*

In the summer of 1971 my son Jonathan and future daughter-in-law Lynne announced that they wanted to get married, but, they said, they weren't sure what type of ceremony they wanted—religious, civil or humanistic. After I got over the shock of hearing this latter unexpected statement, we were able to discuss the formal, unchanging traditional Jewish ceremony that I had been performing for more than thirty years in various formats. It was clear that they wanted a ceremony that would be meaningful to them and reflect their understanding of marriage and mutual obligation. From these discussions there emerged a ceremony that combined the old with the new, the traditional with the modern. They wrote their own introductory words, as well as words for the exchange of rings, plus a concluding portion. All this was interwoven with the parts of the traditional ceremony that I felt were essential. The result was the most emotionally stirring wedding ceremony I have ever been a part of.

This event alerted me to the fact that a growing number of young people are writing part or all of their wedding ceremony. And so I started to collect these custom-made ceremonies, writing to clergy colleagues of all faiths for copies of wedding ceremonies reflecting this new trend.

Shortly afterward, I met Marlene Halpin, who was Academic Dean at Molloy College, Rockville Centre, N.Y., and is now Specialist in Continuing Education for Ministry, and Consultant to the Diocese of Kalamazoo, Michigan, and we discussed this new approach. As dean of a women's college she had helped plan many weddings in which the couple had written a large part of the marriage service and which was easily incorporated into the Catholic Liturgy. This innovation had not only personalized the ceremony but also had enhanced its meaning a thousand-fold. Dr. Halpin shared my enthusiasm for collecting and publishing material that would be helpful to young people who wanted to create their very own wedding service. Thus a partnership was born. A limited amount of material, later expanded for this book, appeared in *Modern Bride,* April–May 1973 issue.

I soon discovered that my good friend, William Genné, marriage and family consultant at the National Council of Churches, had a file of innovative Protestant ceremonies; so he joined us as the third co-editor and author of this book. Thus we are able to offer a book that will be useful to couples of every major faith—Jewish, Roman Catholic or Protestant.

A special word of appreciation is due Mr. Robert R. Wright, managing editor of Association Press, who has helped at every step of the way in seeing this book to fruition.

MORDECAI L. BRILL, *Rabbi*

## A SECOND PERSONAL NOTE

Since this book was first published we have received many letters (plus copies of ceremonies) telling us how much our work helped each couple to plan a personalized, meaningful wedding. We are delighted that our mission was accomplished.

We hope those couples who find this new edition helpful will also send us complete copies of their ceremonies with comments to the address below:

Dr. M. L. Brill
4172 Inverrary Drive
Lauderhill, Fla. 33319

# ACKNOWLEDGMENTS

We are grateful to the friends and acquaintances from whose wedding celebrations we have been permitted to draw many of the materials and suggestions included here.

We owe a special debt of thanks to the many clergypersons and others who have sent us material, and who have encouraged us in the preparation in this book.

# INTRODUCTION

Write your own wedding ceremony? Until recently this would have been unthinkable, but today a growing number of engaged couples are creating their own ceremony, using the traditional format, but infusing it with words, music and ritual that best express the significance of marriage for them. Clergy members want the ceremony to be a highly personalized and meaningful event, and are happy to be active participants in the creation of custom-made ceremonies. The marriage of Patricia Nixon and Edward Cox in June of 1971 reflected this growing trend, for theirs was an "ecumenical ceremony" which they wrote themselves "combining Protestant and Catholic wedding prayers, Biblical verses and other devotional writings."

This resource book will help you create a service of worship appropriate for the occasion. In these pages you will find texts of recent weddings, as well as a collection of the exchange of vows, readings and prayers that will articulate what you feel on that special day. The wedding ceremonies in this book reflect the efforts of many couples just like yourselves. Much thought and preparation went into their work. These are not the last word, but we trust they will stimulate you to achieve a meaningful ceremony of your own. We are certain there will be even more "custom-made" ceremonies in the future.

One college chaplain, disturbed by the sameness of wedding ceremonies, tried new arrangements for seating, a wider selection of music, and new patterns such as having the ceremony follow the wedding dinner. Above all, he insisted on having each couple *participate* in writing and selecting parts of the ceremony, with the bride and groom, as well as others in the wedding party, reading most of the ceremony.

Thus, along with the selection of music and scriptural readings, a couple can create their own liturgy. This is not as difficult as it sounds. Love poems or passages from literature, old and new, are a favorite source of material. "Interwoven with this source material will be affirmations about life and love, about partnership and individuality, about yourself and your place in the community. As simple a question as 'Why do you love him [her]?' will often evoke a response which can easily be adapted into the ceremony."*

Here are some suggestions and questions you might consider when planning your ceremony:

1. Consult first with the officiating clergy member. Enlist her or his co-operation and help. Remember that she/he has to approve of, and be comfortable with, the finished product. Hence, discuss with her/him what parts of the traditional ceremony are a *must*, what parts are *optional.*

2. Some questions: What role do your parents have? Does father "give away" the bride or should both parents share the "giving"? Perhaps you feel "giving away" is outmoded and unnecessary. Should there be a parental blessing?

3. The role of women has changed. Do you use the phrase "love, honor and obey"?

4. Single or double ring ceremony? What do you want to say to your beloved when you present him (her) with the ring?

5. Do you want the best man and maid of honor to participate in the ceremony? Do you want the active participation of all those present through litanies and responsive readings?

---

*Marc Raphael, *The Reconstructionist Magazine,* May 8, 1970.

6. Can you use new symbols or give new meaning to old symbols?

7. How do you want to say thank you to God, to your parents, to all those sharing this wonderful day with you?

8. Fashion a ceremony that fits you, your beliefs and temperament. When participants utter their words with sincerity and fervor the emotional impact on all present can be tremendous.

Modern-day weddings can be a do-it-yourself affair shifting the emphasis from a passive response of "I do" or "I will" to active affirmation. Such ceremonies overcome the feeling many people have that if they've seen one wedding they've seen them all. The challenge you have to face is this: How do you want to proclaim your love to the world? How do you want those sharing your joy to proclaim it? What do you want to say about your future—the new life you undertake together?

Fashioning your own personalized wedding service can be a joyous and exciting experience. Make it your own creation! Make it meaningful to *both of you.* There are many important fringe benefits. For one thing, writing your own ceremony will help both of you to begin communicating your feelings more fully. It will also focus on what each of you truly believes about marriage.

A meaningful marriage begins with a meaningful wedding! The wedding, however, does not have to be a big expensive show. It can be simple and modest. We are equally concerned about spending too much energy on wedding preparations and too little on preparation for marriage, i.e., the post-wedding handling of day-by-day problems and challenges. Hence, we have included in our suggested readings some worthwhile books on preparation for marriage.

The essence of the wedding ceremony is a freely given, publicly proclaimed consent and commitment made before God and people. In this book you will find sections dealing with the essential elements found in the traditional Jewish, Catholic and Protestant ceremonies. Your clergy member can guide you as to what can be omitted, where your own material can fit in, and so on. Needless to say, your wedding ceremony must be in accord with the requirements of your faith group and the laws of your state.

The editors of this book hope that the materials and suggestions found here will help you make your own wedding ceremony a thing of beauty, an unforgettable experience, and a joyful remembrance.

Congratulations and Mazel Tov!

MORDECAI L. BRILL
MARLENE HALPIN
WILLIAM GENNÉ

# THE MEANING
# OF THE WEDDING

Before you plunge into writing your wedding it will help to stand back and look at the grand design. Ask yourself some questions: What is the over-all idea about a wedding? How does it hang together? What is the meaning and purpose of it all?

A cynic has said that the wedding is a meaningless ritual enacted after all the important decisions have been made. While it may be true that the basic decision—so personal, so intimate, so sacred—was made earlier by the couple in private, it does not necessarily follow that the wedding is meaningless. On the contrary, the wedding has some very real meanings of its own and adds several dimensions to the agreement made between the lovers.

The essential heart of the wedding is the vow or covenant (much deeper than a contract) the partners make to each other pledging to do everything in their power to help each other achieve the fullest development possible (despite all obstacles) forever! Now it is one thing to whisper such a pledge in private. A new dimension is added, however, when such a pledge to each other is acknowledged in the presence of family and friends and phrased in the form of a sacred vow. Each partner cannot help but feel reassured and strengthened to receive such a voluntary unconditional public commitment from the other. The wedding ceremony provides a very special way of saying to each other: "I love you!"

True lovers feel good inside and out. They want to sing and dance and shout. They want the whole world to know their great joy. The wedding ceremony can be the dramatic vehicle for communicating all these wonderful feelings to their families, to their friends, and to the whole world and to receive their affirmation. The wedding adds a public dimension to those very intimate vows. There is not only communication but also very real support from the larger group. The more people who share this joy, the more there are who want to see it flourish. All the world loves a lover!

Elopements or secret marriages miss this dimension of community celebration and support which can do so much to enrich and support the couple, especially when the going gets rough.

As you write your wedding you will want to consider not only the vows you make to each other, but also how you can involve other members of your families and friends in ways which dramatically symbolize their joy and support in your great adventure.

The wedding has a third dimension, however, which is beyond the couple themselves and their families and friends because it allows them to give the whole experience a sacred and eternal significance. When a couple make their vows and their prayers to God they are saying to themselves and to all who witness that their love is more than human. They acknowledge that the source of their love is in God and the course of their love is to fulfill God's loving will for their lives and that the goal of their love is to grow in love. By acknowledging the Divine source and power of their love their whole relationship takes on cosmic significance. The power of the universe flows through them not only to enrich each other but to enrich and inspire all who know them.

We do not want to belittle the beauty of the relationships that many young people experience in our contemporary society. However, when some of them say, "What difference can a few prayers make to the way we feel together?" we feel we must challenge them to consider the opportunities they are missing to dramatize, communicate, and share with others the full beauty and power of their relationship. We also feel they are missing powerful sources of strength in themselves and in their communities to enrich and nourish their relationship to its fullest potential.

We also challenge those of you who have this book about weddings to allow your creative spirit full sway to express your love in music, poetry and in an increasing range of symbols from the traditional rings to flowers, fruits and wines, along with other artistic expressions, all to the end that you and your friends will sense the beauty and the power of the love God has placed in your hearts.

We offer you in this book many joyous elements created by others who have trod the pathways of love before you in the hope that they will inspire your love to creative expression in the wedding service you write together. May the writing of your own service set the pattern of creating new ways of working together on all of the great adventures that lie ahead in your marriage.

Our prayers go with you!

# ESSENTIAL ELEMENTS OF THE WEDDING SERVICE

## JEWISH*

The Jewish wedding ceremony is rooted in deepest antiquity and its basic features have remained unchanged for many centuries. Long ago the Rabbis of the Talmud elevated the idea of marriage to a lofty plane by calling it *kiddushin* (sanctification).

As one Jewish scholar has pointed out: "The married state, according to Jewish teaching, is an ideal state. It has been divinely instituted for the happiness of the individual and for the well-being of human society. . . . There is no occasion in life when the divine blessing and guidance are more fitly invoked than on the wedding day when a man and woman take each other, for good or for evil, for weal or for woe. They are henceforth to be the custodians of each other's well-being. The marriage ceremony itself, then, is properly invested with a sacred character; its solemnization appropriately becomes a religious rite."

Though the Rabbinic teachers spoke of the marriage ceremony as "sanctification," it was not a *sacrament* that can never be undone. Thus, in the Jewish ceremony such statements as "until death do us part" or "that which God has put together

---

*Adapted in part from Chapter 17 of *The Jewish Marriage Anthology* by Philip and Hanna Goodman, Jewish Publication Society, 1965.

let no man tear asunder" are never used. Jewish tradition sees marriage as between two imperfect human beings, and hence mistakes are possible and divorce can become a sad reality. This realistic view in no way cheapens the sanctity of marriage in the eyes of Jewish tradition.

The *essence of the ceremony* is the act of espousal which is performed by the bridegroom. He places a ring (which must be his own property) on the bride's forefinger of her right hand— the index finger that points easily— so that she can readily display it for the two witnesses to see as legal evidence of matrimony. The bridegroom then declares: "Behold, thou art consecrated to me with this ring according to the laws of Moses and Israel." This giving and acceptance of the ring knowingly and of one's own free will in the presence of witnesses makes the wedding valid and binding in the eyes of Jewish religious law. All the rest of the ceremony enhances and reinforces this mutual commitment.

*Fasting on the wedding day* until after the ceremony is a time honored tradition. According to the Talmud "when a man marries his sins are forgiven." Hence the wedding day is considered sanctified for bride and groom and is likened to Yom Kippur (Day of Atonement). As Yom Kippur atones for sins, so matrimony brings forgiveness and enables the bridal pair to embark on life together with a "clean slate"—they begin writing a new book of life together.

*Processional.* Although the order of the processional is a matter of local procedure, the custom of escorts for the groom and the bride is quite ancient. The Talmud states that the verse in Genesis (2:22) "And he brought her [Eve] unto the man" teaches that God acted as best man for Adam. Furthermore, since the bridal couple is compared to a king and queen, it is fitting that they have entourages. In a traditional ceremony the groom's parents escort him and the bride's parents accompany her to the canopy.

The bride stands under the canopy at the groom's right, for as the Psalmist said: "At thy right hand doth a queen stand." (Psalm 45:10). The bride is a queen on her wedding day.

*Huppah (canopy).* The wedding service, even when performed inside the synagogue, takes place under a canopy, usually made of silk or velvet, supported by four staves. The original meaning of the Hebrew word Huppah was "room" or "covering." It is symbolic of the couple's new home.

In earlier times the Huppah was a wedding tent or chamber. The Talmud tells us that when a boy was born, a cedar tree was planted, and at the birth of a girl an acacia tree was planted. When they grew up and were to be married, the trees were cut down and used for their wedding canopy.

*Ketubah.* The Ketubah is a "marriage contract," the only documentary evidence (prior to modern times) of the validity of the marriage. Orthodox and Conservative Rabbis still use a traditional Ketubah, properly witnessed, which they hand over to the bride after reading all or part of it during the ceremony.

Reform Rabbis may or may not use a Ketubah. A new Reform Ketubah, recently formulated by a Rabbinical committee on Reform Jewish practice, is now available.

The Ketubah specifies the obligations the groom assumes for the care of his bride and the settlement he must provide in the event she is widowed or divorced. Prior to modern civil laws, the Ketubah provided protection and future security for the wife.

The English text of the Ketubah (paraphrased from the Aramaic) reads as follows:

This Certificate Witnesseth that
On the _____ day of the week, the _____ day of the month _____ in the year 57 ___ corresponding to the _____ day of _____, 19___, the holy Covenant of Marriage was entered into at _____ between the Bridegroom _____
and his Bride _____

The said Bridegroom made the following
declaration to his Bride:
"Be thou my wife according to the law of Moses and
Israel. I faithfully promise that I will be a true husband
unto thee. I will honor and cherish thee, protect and
support thee, and provide all that is necessary for thy
due sustenance, even as it becometh a Jewish husband
to do. I also take upon myself all such further obligations
for thy maintenance, during thy life-time, as are prescribed by our religious statute."

And the said Bride has plighted her troth unto him,
in affection and in sincerity, and has thus taken upon
herself the fulfilment of all the duties incumbent upon a
Jewish wife.

This Covenant of Marriage was duly executed and
witnessed this day, according to the usage of Israel.

_____ Bridegroom
_____ Bride
_____ Rabbi
_____ Witness
_____ Witness

*Two cups of wine.* During the ceremony the bride and groom
partake of two goblets of wine. The goblets symbolize the cups
of joy and sorrow; thereby the couple express their readiness to
share life's joys and difficulties, "carving life's destiny together."

*Breaking of the glass.* At the conclusion of the ceremony it is
traditional for the bridegroom to break a thin wineglass by
stamping upon it with his foot. There are many explanations and
symbolisms attached to this ceremony. In order to avoid
extreme levity and drunken revelry, the Rabbis in Talmudic
times sometimes broke an expensive goblet to temper uncon-
trolled levity. The loss of a glass was a burden, since glass was
quite expensive in those days.

At a later time the broken glass was a reminder of the
destruction of the Temple in Jerusalem. Thus, even at a time of
highest happiness (exultant wedding joy) we recall the great
calamity that befell the Jewish people long ago and remind the
bridal couple of the sorrows of Israel.

Other explanations have been given for this custom. It is considered a warning to the bridal pair of the frailty and transitoriness of life. Just as one blow can shatter a glass, so the sanctity and harmony of the home can be destroyed by a single act of thoughtlessness or infidelity. As easy as it is to break a glass, so petty squabbles and arguments or quick temper may lead to the breakup of a marriage.

The breaking of a glass also symbolizes irrevocability. Just as this is an irrevocable act so, too, marriage should be unchangeable and permanent.

Some Reform Rabbis do not require a Huppah. Similarly, they often omit the second cup of wine and the breaking of the glass.

# ROMAN CATHOLIC

At the heart of marriage, for Roman Catholics, is that it is a "covenant, by which a man and a woman establish between themselves a partnership of the whole of life." (New Code of Canon Law, Canon #1055). This marriage covenant between baptized persons is known as a sacrament for Catholics. By its nature it is for the good of the spouses, and for the procreation and education of children. The "marriage is brought about through the *consent* of the parites, legitimately manifested between persons who are capable according to law of giving consent." (Canon 1057).

Because weddings have profound religious significance for the community, and because they are such important beginnings of new life, most religions have developed teachings, ceremonies and symbols about marriage. The Catholic Church holds that, when validly baptized persons marry, there is always the sacrament of matrimony in addition to the natural marriage contract. This is a lovely thing to talk about, to understand, to realize.

Catholics celebrate the high points of life in liturgical ceremonies. These rituals— both sign and reality— express to all present what is, in fact, happening. In baptism the individual person enters the community redeemed by Jesus and of which

He is head. Confirmation completes the initiation as the Christian community prays that the persons be animated by the Spirit, that they witness to others what they have received. In Eucharist the whole community celebrates the mystery of Jesus in their lives, continuing and deepening that faith begun in baptism. In reconciliation the community celebrates forgiving and healing. Also, the sacrament is an aid in our continuing reconciliation with God and the human community. Anointing focuses the care and concern of the community toward those who suffer from sickness or old age. When a new family is to begin, when new love gives promise of new life, there is cause for another celebration—marriage. Here is experienced and expressed the most committed of friendships, conjugal love. And here, too, as in all of life's most important moments, we want the sacramental presence of God.

Words alone do not express the love of the couple adequately. The mysterious sacredness, the profound spiritual reality of marriage— beyond communication to communion— is signified by fidelity: the creative fidelity of God to His people; of Jesus to His Church; of man to his wife— and of woman to her husband. It is shared mystery, shared sacredness, shared love, shared loyalty. At the wedding it is promised and revealed: to and for the church and the community of all people.

However the couple agree to "share bed, board and dwelling," however they express their down-deep worship of each other, the couple truly is starting a new life. In many ways— great and small— each one dies to personal preferences: in life style, friends, in diet, entertainment, even some priorities and values. Each one sacrifices something to create this new life, which— when well lived— gives each a strength and perhaps compassion, neither would have alone. At the wedding the man and woman promise to spend a life-time learning and living this "two becoming one."

As the creating God is life-giving, so are the couple whose sacramental marriage is witness to the love of God for His people, the love of Christ for the Church. Intimacy between the couple expands to intimacy of the family and blooms into hospitality. Hospitality of heart and of home is extended to

27

those who approach them, or to whom they extend themselves in love and compassion. Marriage calls for large hearts: to make room for each other, to make room for loved and needy others.

Since the fourth or fifth century, Catholic couples have been encouraged to marry during the celebration of Eucharist. In this central act of worship of the Catholic faith there are many appropriate points when the man and woman can share in word, music, ceremony, their hopes and dreams with each other. And with the people they love best. Eucharist is not essential to the wedding, but it lends its own happy dimensions for that celebration. During the liturgy, Jesus, in love, gives His Body and Blood for us. During the marriage ceremony, the man and woman covenant their lives to each other in love.

Soon after your engagement, speak to a priest, deacon or pastoral associate. Since the wedding generally is in the bride's parish, it is good to find out early how diverse are the liturgical practices current in parish or diocese. Canonically, the pastor of the bride has the right to preside at the wedding ceremony. If you want another priest to preside (for example, a family member or particularly close friend), it is required to request the bride's pastor to delegate the other priest. Discuss the liturgy, music, original prayers (*e. g.,* prayer of the faithful appropriate to the families and friends involved), and use of symbols that best express your faith, feelings, hopes and dreams with each other in the presence of God and your people. Discuss these things with each other and your priest well before the wedding. It would be well to remember that the present approved rituals allow for some diversity in the ceremony. Should your pastor (or priest delegated by him in the parish) be unwilling to use the permitted options within the ceremony, and if it is important to you, remember that you have legitimate recourse. Speak to a priest who will be able to deal with the appropriate official in the diocesan chancery and ask about diocesan policies. The ceremony should be conducted according to your wishes if you remember to keep in mind the sacramental reality of marriage, church law, and good taste.

In the pages which follow there are examples—not only of

how couples today are wording their vows to each other in terms meaningful to them and relevant to their world—but also of the unique prayers and ceremonies throughout the liturgy. These adaptations are not just for *a* wedding liturgy, but for *this couple's wedding:* written particularly as their own private expression of their love and commitment. Each is different. Each is moving. Each is "right" for that couple. We hope that these examples of how others understand and express their marriage vows will help you to think through your own marriage ceremony and share the enjoyment and love of creating your own wedding day.

## PROTESTANT

Protestant denominations vary in their ideas about weddings from the strictly sacramental and liturgical (prescribed form and words) to a great freedom in the form and words a couple may use.

Our suggestion is that you consult your pastor at the earliest possible moment to learn the official practice of the church you want to bless your wedding. Most pastors are willing, even eager, to help couples express in honest, meaningful ways their convenant of marriage.

The heart of the wedding is the vows the couple take to each other. This is the central part, around which all else is built. The laws of our society require that these vows be taken in the presence of a legally recognized officiant, either a magistrate for a civil service or a clergyman for a religious service. The laws also require two witnesses and a license to wed which certifies that certain preconditions, such as age of responsibility, have been met. Each state establishes its own marriage laws, however, and specific requirements will vary from state to state.

Because our churches and pastors have been working for centuries to help couples enjoy success in their marriages, they have accumulated much knowledge about the conditions that promote a successful marriage. It is these conditions which should be included in some form in the vows which are expressed.

Pastors know that it is a dangerous sign if a couple want to enter marriage with "their fingers crossed"—that is, with mental reservations about their commitment to each other. This is why the community of faith expects an honest pledge to lifelong fidelity: "In sickness or in health; in poverty or in wealth." A successful marriage cannot be only a fair-weather arrangement.

One of the encouraging signs in many modern weddings is that couples are no longer content to pledge themselves to help each other; they also pledge to work together on the great issues of life in our society, such as racial and economic justice, brotherhood and peace. This dedication to a purpose larger than just their own happiness is a vital element in the growth and strength of a marriage.

Pastors know that a large, expensive ceremony does not ensure a good marriage. Most pastors will be eager to help you plan a beautiful, meaningful ceremony at minimum expense. Elaborate receptions are not necessary. The ceremony and reception can be planned in the church or at home, since these are the two most sacred places in our lives.

The following pages suggest many ideas and symbols that can be built around the wedding vows to enrich their meaning. Processionals, music, rings, the joining of hands and many other symbols—old and new—and the Lord's Supper can be incorporated to express the meaning desired by the couple.

As with any other art form, the wedding will often attain most beauty and power through simplicity and sincerity. You do not need to have freaky clothes and rituals to make your wedding modern and relevant. What you want to say to each other and to your family and friends will come through loud and clear without distractions.

Only couples who are willing to work hard to build their marriage are encouraged to seek the blessing of their church. Success is ensured only by the total, highest commitment of the couple. It is to this commitment that the community of faith adds its loving prayers and support.

# *THREE CONTEMPORARY CELEBRATIONS*

### JEWISH

Our Wedding—Joyce and David

PROCESSIONAL: Cantor or soloist sing each of the processional songs as the parties indicated below walk down the aisle. As they get halfway to the Huppah, the soloist shifts to declaiming the paraphrase and then back to singing.

1. For male attendants: "Hineh mah tov u-mah naim"

   How good, how pleasant it is
   for all of us to be here together.

2. For groom and parents: "Eleh hamdah libbi"

   This is what my heart desires;
   Joyous love that lasts forever.

3. For female attendants: "Erev shel shosamim"

   It is a time for flowers
   A time for songs of love.

4. For bride and parents: "Ha-naavah ba-banot"

   O my lovely bride,
       Let me gaze upon your face;

> Come to me, my beloved,
> > And stay with me always.

5. For groom to escort bride to Huppah: "Simi yadekh be-yadi"

   Put your hand in mine;
   I am yours and you are mine.

WELCOME (*from Bride and Groom—or officiating Rabbi*) See pp 56–60 for suggestions.

BLESSING OVER THE FIRST CUP OF WINE (*Rabbi*)

THE BETROTHAL CEREMONY: Hosea 2:21–22 (*music by David Shneyer*)

Bride and Groom

V'eyrastich li L'Olam
V'eyrastich li L'Olam
V'eyrastich li b'tzedek u-b'mishpat
u'v'chesed u'v-rachamim (2)
V'eyrastich li be-emunah
V'yadat et Adonai.

"And I will betroth you unto Me forever; Yea, I will betroth you unto Me in righteousness, and in justice, and in loving-kindness, and in compassion. And I will betroth you unto Me in faithfulness; And you shall know Adonai."

OUR VOWS (*Bride or Groom*)

We share so much together that we want to marry and to share some of that joy with others. We both sense a common bond among all human beings and from that grows a reverence for life which guides us in our relationships with others—most of all with each other.

With these rings we join our lives and promise to go on loving, trusting, and sharing our lives for all time.

32

(The groom places the ring on bride's finger and says:)
"Harei ot m'kudeshet li b'taba-at zu k'dat Moshe v'Yisrael"

Joyce, I give you this ring as a symbol of my love, precious and without end. I give you this ring as I give you my love.

(The bride then gives the groom a ring and says:)
"Harei attah mekudash li b'taba-at zu kedat Moshe v'Yisrael"

David, I give you this ring as a symbol of my love, precious and without end. I give you this ring as I give you my love.

SONG: Psalm 100 (*or other suitable music*)—(*All*)

READING OF THE MARRIAGE CONTRACT(*Ketubah*)—(*All or part Rabbi*)

(Each couple can compose a document of mutual obligations. The following is an example.)

We, _____ (Hebrew and English names) and _____ have covenanted to enter into Jewish marriage according to the laws of Moses and Israel. We pledge to God and to each other that we shall keep the love which unites us sacred, cherishing each other always, ever sensitive to one another's qualities, and forebearing of one another's shortcomings. When either of us attains the joy of personal fulfillment, may we rejoice together; when either one is disquieted by frustration, may our mutual love and support be a source of strength and peace.

We shall endeavor to understand clearly not only the words that come from the lips but, of greater importance, the feelings and aspirations that stir our hearts.

Mindful of the Biblical admonition that "unless the Lord build the house, its builders labor in vain," we shall strive to make the Presence of God and the value of Jewish tradition evident in our home.

United in marriage, may we serve others ever more effectively and help build the better world of tomorrow.

33

Signed in＿＿＿＿＿＿＿＿ , this＿＿＿＿＿＿＿ day of
(Hebrew month and year) corresponding to the
(English date)


＿＿＿＿＿＿＿＿＿＿    ＿＿＿＿＿＿＿＿＿＿＿

Bridegroom              ' Bride

Witnesses ＿＿＿＿＿＿＿＿＿＿＿＿＿＿＿＿＿

＿＿＿＿＿＿＿＿＿＿＿＿＿＿＿＿＿＿＿

＿＿＿＿＿＿＿＿＿＿＿＿＿＿＿＿＿ Rabbi

SOLO

SECOND CUP OF WINE

CHANTING OF SEVEN BLESSINGS (Sheva Berahot)—(*Rabbi or Cantor*)

Blessed are You, O Lord our God, Ruler of the Universe, who created all things for Your glory.

Blessed are You, O Lord our God, King of the Universe, Creator of all Your children.

Blessed are You, O Lord our God, Ruler of the Universe who has established marriage for the fulfillment and perpetuation of life in accordance with Your holy purpose.

Blessed are You, O Lord our God, Ruler of the Universe, who are the source of all gladness and joy. Through your grace we attain affection, companionship and peace.

Grant, O Lord, that the love which unites＿＿＿＿＿ and ＿＿＿＿＿ , bridegroom and bride, may grow in abiding happiness. May they always have faith in their marriage, sustained and ennobled by their devotion to Jewish ideals and teachings.

May there be serenity in their home, peace and confidence

34

in their hearts. May they be guided by Your Divine
Presence. Blessed are You, O Lord, who consecrates
bridegroom and bride to each other.

BREAKING OF GLASS

BENEDICTION *(Rabbi, or Parents jointly)*

RECESSIONAL Suggested melody: "Od Yishama be-arei yehudah
u-vechutzot Yerushalyim"

May there always be heard in the cities of Judah
and in the streets of Jerusalem the voice of gladness
and the voice of joy, the voice of the bridegroom and
the voice of the bride.

(Play instrumentally)

All sing: "Siman Tov"

Siman tov umazel tov, umazel tov vesiman tov (3)
yehei lanu . . . ulechol am Yisrael.

A good sign and good luck for us and for the entire people of
Israel.


# ROMAN CATHOLIC


## ENTRANCE AND RITE OF WELCOME
*(Congregation stands)*
PROCESSIONAL *(Pachelbel, Johann Canon in D major "Celebrated
Canon"—Concordia")*

WELCOME
*(Spoken by Priest)*

We welcome Jennifer and Doug, their families and friends,
to this celebration of their love. We thank God for Doug's
and Jen's parents, Doug's grandparents, all of you—their
relatives and friends—who helped them grow into the

maturity and love of this holy, happy day. Let us ask God to bless their new life and let us who love them add our blessing.

OPENING PRAYERS (greeting, penitential rite, litany)
(*Priest, with responses by all*):

Let us begin in the name of the Father and of the Son and of the Holy Spirit.

*Amen.*

The grace of our Lord Jesus Christ and the Love of God and the fellowship of the Holy Spirit be with you all.

*And also with you.*

My brothers and sisters, today we celebrate the love of Jennifer and Doug. To prepare ourselves to celebrate this and the sacred mysteries let us call to mind the times when we have sinned and not loved enough.

Lord, we have sinned against You, by being impatient and selfish, by not trusting You and each other,

*Lord, have mercy.*

Lord, you have seen us love You and others too little,

*Lord, have mercy.*

Lord, make your mercy and love real in our lives,

*And grant us your salvation.*

May almighty God have mercy on us, forgive us our sins, and bring us to eternal life.

*Amen.*

GLORIA

PRAYER (Philippians 4:4–9)

Let us pray, with St. Paul: Jennifer and Doug, I want you to be happy, always happy in the Lord; I repeat, what I want is your happiness. Let your tolerance be evident to everyone: the Lord is very near. There is no need to worry; but if there is anything you need, pray for it, asking God for it with prayer and thanksgiving, and that peace of God, which is so much greater than we can understand, will guard your hearts and your thoughts, in Christ Jesus. Finally, Jennifer and Doug, fill your minds with everything that is true, good and pure, everything that we love and honor, and everything that can be thought virtuous or worthy of praise. Then the God of peace will be with you, through Christ our Lord. *Amen.*

## LITURGY OF THE WORD

(*Congregation seated*)

FIRST READING (Book of Wisdom 7:7–14)
(*By family member or guest.*) *At end of which the reader shall say:*

This is the word of the Lord.

(*All*) *Thanks be to God.*

MUSIC (*optional*)

RESPONSORIAL PSALM (Psalm 136—Litany of Thanksgiving)
(*Led by family member or guest, with responses by all.*)

His love is everlasting!

*Alleluia!*

Give thanks to God, for He is good.

*His love is everlasting!*

Give thanks to the Lord of lords.

*His love is everlasting!*

He alone performs great marvels.

*His love is everlasting!*

His wisdom made the heavens.

*His love is everlasting!*

He set the earth on the waters.

*His love is everlasting!*

He provides for all living creatures.

*His love is everlasting!*

Give thanks to the God of Heaven.

*His love is everlasting!*

SECOND READING (John 3:19–24)
*(By family member or guest.) At end of which the reader shall say:*

This is the word of the Lord.

*(All) Thanks be to God.*

*(Congregation stands)*

GOSPEL
*(Proclaimed by Priest, with responses by all.)*

Alleluia, alleluia, alleluia

*Alleluia, alleluia, alleluia*

Be faithful unto death, says the Lord,
and I will give you the crown of life.

*Alleluia, alleluia, alleluia*

The Lord be with you.

*And also with you.*

A reading taken from the holy Gospel
according to Mark 10:6–9.

*Glory to you, Lord.*

*Reading of the Gospel passages.*
*At the end of the Gospel the priest shall say:*

This is the Gospel of the Lord.

*(All) Praise to You, Lord Jesus Christ.*

HOMILY

PROFESSION OF FAITH (Nicene Creed)
*(Recited by All if the day's liturgy calls for it.)*

## RITE OF MARRIAGE

*(Congregation sits)*

MARRIAGE EXHORTATION *(By the Celebrant)*

Jennifer and Doug, you have come together in this church so that the Lord may seal and strengthen your love in the presence of the Church's minister and this community. Christ abundantly blesses this love. He has already consecrated you in baptism, and now He enriches and strengthens you by a special sacrament so that you may assume the duties of marriage in mutual and lasting fidelity. And so, in the presence of the Church, I ask you to state your intentions.

EXCHANGE OF VOWS

*Doug:* Jennifer, today I give myself to you and ask for your tomorrows. I promise to love you more than anyone else can; to give you my strength, and ask for yours in return, to help you in good times and in bad. I give you all my trust and ask you to accept me as your husband.

*Jennifer:* Yes, I will.

*Jennifer:* Doug, today I promise to love and honor you all my life; to give you my strength; to stand by you in joy and in sorrow and ask you to stand by me. I pray that our home will be one of love and understanding. I give you all my trust, all my tomorrows and ask you to accept me as your wife.

*Doug:* Yes, I will.

*Best Man and*
*Maid of Honor:* We have heard Doug and Jennifer pledge themselves to God and each other in marriage. Before God and this community we witness that Doug and Jennifer are husband and wife.

*All:* We, your family and friends, witness that you have accepted each other as husband and wife. We welcome you as a new family into our community and we praise God for your love.

*Priest:* By the authority of the Church I ratify and bless the bond of marriage you have covenanted.

In the Name of the Father and of the Son and of the Holy Spirit.

*All:* Amen.

BLESSINGS AND EXCHANGE OF RINGS

*Priest:* Heavenly Father, bless these rings. Grant that Jennifer and Doug may wear them with deep faith in each other. May they do your will and always live together in peace, love and abiding joy. We ask this through Christ our Lord.

*All:* Amen.

*Doug:* Jennifer, wear this ring as a sign of my love and the giving that will last the rest of my life.

*Jennifer:* Doug, take this ring as a sign of my love and the giving that will last the rest of my life.

BLESSING OF THE COUPLE

*Priest:* Lord, bless and consecrate Jennifer and Doug in their love for each other. May the rings they have exchanged be a reminder of the love and faithfulness they have pledged to each other.

*All:* Amen.

RITE OF PEACE

(*If the congregation is not too large*)

*Priest:* Let us greet Doug and Jennifer, and each other, with a sign of the peace of Christ.

# GENERAL INTERCESSION

(*Congregation stands*)

(*While the liturgy of the Eucharist is largely prescribed, it offers certain opportunities for spontaneity and participation, as this service indicates. We strongly encourage the bridal couple to write this prayer, including those dear to them both present and absent. If a loved one is unable to attend because of illness, distance, and so on, taping the ceremony is a lovely way to include them.*)

PRAYER OF THE FAITHFUL

*Priest:* May the love of Jennifer and Doug, which has brought them together and led them to make this marriage covenant, grow stronger as they live their life together.

*All:* Grant them this grace, O Lord, we lovingly pray.

*Family Member or Guest:* May Jennifer's and Doug's Christian marriage begin with happiness and endure in peace,

*All:* Grant them this grace, O Lord, we lovingly pray.

*Family Member or Guest:* May all present be inspired by the love of Jennifer and Doug and by their faith in the future that enables them to begin a new family,

*All:* Grant us this grace, O Lord, we lovingly pray.

*Family Member or Guest:* May Doug find in Jennifer's people a new family in which he may be a good son,

*All:* Grant him this grace, O Lord, we lovingly pray.

*Family Member or Guest:* May Jennifer find in Doug's people a new family in which she may be a good daughter,

*All:* Grant her this grace, O Lord, we lovingly pray.

*Family Member or Guest:* May all couples present renew their fidelity to each other through the joy of this celebration.

*All:* Grant us this grace, O Lord, we lovingly pray.

*Priest:* By the grace of the Spirit, God, you give all men the gift of loving. Grant a great increase of this gift to Jennifer and Doug and to all here today, so that we may truly be known by our love.

Through Christ, Our Lord.

*All:* Amen.

*Doug brings Jennifer's mother a rose. Jennifer brings Doug's mother a rose.*

*Family Member or Guest:* May all people find peace in the love of God.

*All:* Grant us this grace, O Lord, we lovingly pray.

## LITURGY OF EUCHARIST

(*Congregation sits*)

OFFERTORY PROCESSION (*music optional—I Have Loved You.* Michael Joncas. NALR or Vol. 2 of *Glory and Praise*).

*Jennifer's and Doug's parents bring to the altar the bread and wine for the Eucharist. We prepare our hearts in silence as the Lord's table is set.*

OFFERTORY PRAYERS

INVITATION TO PRAYER

PRAYER OVER THE GIFTS

INTRODUCTORY DIALOGUE

PREFACE TO EUCHARISTIC PRAYER

ACCLAMATION

# COMMUNION RITE

(*Congregation stands*)

NUPTIAL BLESSING All present raise hands in blessing with the priest.

*Priest:* Let us pray for Doug and Jennifer, who come before our God at the beginning of their married life, so that they will always be in love with each other.

(*Pause for silent prayer*)

*Priest:* O God, our Father, let the depth of love between Jennifer and Douglas be a sign to us, your people, of your faithful love for us.

Bless Jennifer, your daughter, that she may be a faithful and loving wife to Douglas. May her creative love enable her to mother a happy family.

Bless Douglas, your son, that he may be a faithful and loving husband to Jennifer. May his creative love enable him to father a happy family.

We ask you this in the Name of our Lord, your Son, Jesus Christ.

*All:* Amen.

RITE OF PEACE

COMMUNION HYMNS (Reception of Communion—*music optional*)

POST COMMUNION PRAYER

(*Congregation sits*)

*Priest:* God, we have shared with Doug and Jennifer the gift of yourself in the Eucharist. We pray for them now, that they may always be close to You and to each other.

May their love for each other witness to the world that they are Your disciples.

This we ask through Jesus Christ, our Lord.

*All:* Amen.

PRAYER OF THE COUPLE

*Jennifer:* I praise you, O Lord,
I rejoice in you, my Savior!
During all my life you have cared for me,
And brought me to this day.
How holy is your name!
Through your grace I met Doug and offered him
my love;
Through your grace he has accepted it and become
my husband.
Today and forever may I be thankful for this blessing.

*Doug:* I am a man whom God has blessed!
He has given me a treasure more precious than pearl.
Through his grace I met Jennifer and offered her my
love;
Through his grace she has accepted it and become
my wife.

44

Happy the husband of a good wife!
Whether rich or poor, his heart is glad;
　his face speaks his joy.
O Lord, I praise your name and ask you to bless us.

*All:* Jennifer and Doug, we are here to celebrate and
rejoice with you.
We, a community of the people of God,
　bless you and ask his blessing upon you.
May the Lord bless and protect you,
May he make his face to shine upon you and be
　gracious to you;
May the Lord lift up his face to you and make you
　prosper.
May your children bless and honor you;
May your love be as true and as deep as the love of
　Christ for us.
May your love be a sign for us.


## CONCLUDING RITE

*Priest:* The Lord be with you.

*All:* And also with you.

FINAL BLESSING (Philippians 2:1–3)

*Priest:* Let us pray for Doug and Jennifer in the words of St.
Paul:

If our life in Christ means anything to you, if love can
persuade at all, or the Spirit that we have in common, or any
tenderness and sympathy, then be united in your convictions
and united in your love, with a common purpose and a
common mind. Fill the world with the Spirit of Christ, and in
all things, and in the very midst of human affairs, become a
witness of Christ. That is the one thing which would make us
completely happy for you.

*All:* Thanks be to God.

*Priest:* May God our Father keep you in love with each other, so that the peace of Christ may abide with you and to all who share your home.

*All:* Amen.

RECESSIONAL "Sing a New Song." (ps. 93) Don Schutte, NALR.

# PROTESTANT

*(A printed order of service was used, on the front cover of which were printed "Two Lives, One Love.")*

PRELUDES

"Sheep May Safely Graze"                    J. S. Bach
"Jesu, Joy of Man's Desiring"
"Prelude and Fugue in G Minor"

"Canon in D"                                 Pachelbel

PROCESSIONAL

"Trumpet Voluntary in D"                     Purcell

WELCOME TO THE GUESTS                    *(By the Pastor)*

Norman and Elizabeth welcome you, their families and their friends. Each of you has given something of yourself into their lives. They want you to know that your love, guidance and encouragement will forever be appreciated. It is fitting, then, that you should share today in this celebration of their commitment to God and to each other to live their lives as one.

CONCERNING MARRIAGE

Marriage is a gift of God, sealed by a sacred covenant. Norman and Elizabeth have thought about and talked about what marriage means to them. They have learned that a commitment to love each other forever is not entered into lightly. They know that even as they look forward to the happiness that their lives together can bring, it will require understanding and patience and forgiveness.

Norman and Elizabeth come together from different backgrounds and experiences. In the covenant of marriage they do not leave those behind but, instead, form a new family which will broaden the circle of love in this world. Their pledge to be a family and their confidence in the future brings them before us today to enter into this covenant.

SCRIPTURE: I Corinthians 13:1–13

PUBLIC VOWS (*The couple turn and face the congregation.*)

The Congregation (*in unison*): Norman and Elizabeth, do you pledge to love and to support each other at all times; to share both joys and sorrows; to give support when it is needed and encouragement when spirits are low; to be each other's best friend as well as understanding lover?

*Norman and Elizabeth:* We do.

*The Congregation:* Do you pledge to love and respect each other at all times throughout your lives; to never take each other for granted; to allow and encourage each other to grow as persons, thereby enriching your love and deepening your understanding of one another?

*Norman and Elizabeth:* We do.

*The Congregation:* And do you pledge to share your love and the joys of your marriage with all those around you so that they may learn from your love and be encouraged to grow in their own lives?

*Norman and Elizabeth:* We do.

 HYMN: "O Thou Whose Favor Hallows All Occasions"

O Thou whose favor hallows all occasions,
  be present at this convenanting rite;
May every pledge of true and lasting purpose
  be consecrated in thy holy sight.
Confer on those before thee heavenly aid
  to keep the solemn vows that here are made.

Long may they keep the sense of high adventure,
  the gift of joy, the marvel of a dream,
Nor ever lose the vision as they cherish
  each for the other, honor and esteem.
Enrich them with the blessing of thy grace,
  and make their home Thy constant dwelling place.

Almighty God, redeemer and defender,
  by Thou our stay whatever may betide;
Increasingly may each new year discover
  their lives matured, their marriage sanctified,
Their hearts firm fixed on this exalted goal;
  the praise of God whose name their vows extol.

PRIVATE VOWS (*The couple will each take a lighted candle from a stand near their parents pews and go up into the chancel and, placing the candle on the altar, turn and face each other and join hands.*)

*Norman to Elizabeth:* I, Norman, take thee, Elizabeth, to be my wedded wife, to have and to hold from this day forward, for better for worse, for richer for poorer, in sickness and in health, to love and to cherish, 'til death us do part, according to God's holy ordinance, and thereto I give thee my love.

*Elizabeth to Norman:* I, Elizabeth, take thee, Norman, to be my wedded husband, to have and to hold from this day forward, for better for worse, for richer for poorer, in sickness and in health, to love and to cherish, 'til death us do part, according to God's holy ordinance, and thereto I give thee my love.

GIVING AND RECEIVING OF RINGS

*Pastor:* What symbols are given of the covenant between Norman and Beth are given?

The ring is an ancient symbol which stands for God, eternity, and God's eternal love. The ring is an appropriate symbol because it has no beginning and no end. These rings are symbols of that eternal love in which we share and are symbols of the covenant of love which Beth and Norman have made. May their love be like these rings, remembering no beginning and seeing no end to their love, and may God bless these rings and the relationship which they symbolize.

Norman (*putting ring on Elizabeth's finger*): In the presence of God and all assembled here, I offer you this ring as a symbol of the never-ending love and respect that I will always have for you and for our relationship.

Accept it as a symbol of my desire for us to become one— one love, one life and one family made from the dreams, hopes and hearts of two.

I commit myself to working at this relationship so that it will continue to grow, enriching our love and our lives from this day forward for as long as I shall live.

Elizabeth (*putting ring on Norman's finger*): In the presence of God and all assembled here, I offer you this ring as a symbol of the never-ending love and respect that I will always have for you and for our relationship.

Accept it as a symbol of my desire for us to become one— one love, one life and one family, made from the dreams, hopes and hearts of two.

I commit myself to working at this relationship so that it will continue to grow, enriching our love and our lives from this day forward for as long as I shall live.

BENEDICTION

*Pastor:* Now you will feel no rain, for each of you

will be shelter for the other.
Now you will feel not cold, for each of you
   will be warmth to the other.
Now you are two persons, but there is only
   one life before you.
Go now to your dwelling place, to enter
   into the days of your life together,) (togetherness
And may your days be good and long upon the earth.

Now go in peace and live in love, sharing the most precious gifts you have—the gifts of your lives. May the blessing of God the Creator, God the Redeemer and God the Renewer be with you to guide you this day and forevermore. *Amen.*

CHIMES (*as the bride and groom kiss*)

RECESSIONAL

**Wedding March from "A Midsummer Night's Dream"**
**Felix Mendelssohn**

# A COLLECTION
# OF RESOURCES

## OPENING WORDS

*Instead of a formal address to the congregation, many a clergyperson today begins the wedding celebration with a few informal opening words, either written by him/herself or by the couple being married. It is a warm and welcome act to include and thank all who helped bring the couple to this day.*

Dear friends, out of affection for Joan and Russ we have gathered together to witness and bless their mutual vows which will unite them in marriage. To this moment they bring the fullness of their hearts as a treasure to share with one another. They bring the dreams which bind them together. They bring that particular personality and spirit which is uniquely their own, and out of which will grow the reality of their life together. We rejoice with them as the outward symbol of an inward union of hearts, a union created by friendship, respect and love.

No person should attend a wedding without giving thanks to God for the institution of marriage, and renewing in his heart the vows that are being taken for the first time by others.

No person should leave without doing that for which he came... praying that God's blessing may truly rest upon this man and this woman all the days of their life together.

As you pray, so may you also receive a blessing.

You have been invited to share in a happy and holy occasion—the wedding service. This is a service of worship in which a covenant is established between husband and wife in the presence of God. You are present to join, always inwardly and sometimes audibly, in this act of worship. Perhaps you are already married. For you this may be a time of remembrance and renewal of vows. Perhaps you are contemplating marriage. Then join with us in this place of prayer, where we shall all be reminded that marriage is divinely ordained and is to be kept sacred through joy and adversity. This is an hour of worship, dedicated to God. The presence of his Spirit during this service depends in part upon your preparation and participation. As you wait, we invite you to meditate and pray, letting these words call you to worship:

> Know ye that the Lord he is God;
> It is he that hath made us,
> And not we ourselves;
> We are his people,
> And the sheep of his pasture.
> Enter into his gates with thanksgiving,
> And into his courts with praise;
> Be thankful unto him,
> And bless his name.
> For the Lord is good;
> His mercy is everlasting;
> And his truth endureth to all
> generations.
>
> —PSALM 100:3–5

We have come together today into a community of love, to witness and support the marriage of Margery and Blain before God. We celebrate this occasion through worship, which is both solemn and joyful. It is solemn because it is established in prayerful obedience to the Will of God, which is that man and woman should become a union of two persons. This worship is also solemn because it involves a covenant between these two which is made in the presence of God and the gathered community. This is a joyful time, however, for now a love will have taken a great step toward fulfillment, and a pattern of living will be developed between these two whereby their response to God's love in Christ may be worked out to please him in all the new and creative ways that marriage can bring.

Therefore, this adventure must begin with only the utmost of honesty existing between these two and among you who witness this event. Be it known to you all that the responsibility for the integrity with which Blain and Margery make this covenant finally rests upon their own hearts and the members of this community, both friends and relatives who have ministered to them in the times preparatory to this service.

If you desire this new estate to be permanent, then cherish the vision of this love. Let it not be tarnished by the common events. Believe in this ideal you both share. It is binding; it is inviolate and, in all human relations, it is the final truth.

Love is an Eternal Triangle. God is at the apex and man and woman are at the base of the triangle. When man and woman are joined together with God at the top, they will not be separated from each other at the bottom.

In genuine love two persons look out together in the same direction and direct their lives together toward common ideals and goals.

As Christians, we look upon the ceremony not as a spectacle, but as a worship celebration. It is the highest we know in love—the pledging of the deepest faith and fidelity each to the other, and the expression of their highest aspirations. It is sacred for the two persons being united in marriage, a reenactment for others, and for all of us a mutual sharing and responsibility in this holy marriage.

Tom and Brenda have invited their family and friends to share in this experience as they affirm each other as life partners and as they establish a home and fulfill life together. The words, "I love you," first spoken shyly four years ago are today spoken in full commitment to each other and with adult responsibility to society.

As we share with them in this celebration of worship and love, may we all grow in love and joy.

*Minister:* Bruce and Barbara have invited us to share in the celebration of one of life's most sacred relationships, wherein they covenant to guard the welfare of the other more carefully than their own; they affirm their love before the altar of God; they pledge their faith to one another and they enter into the joys and privileges of marriage.

*Congregation:* As they give themselves each to the other in love, we pray that their hopes may be realized.

*Minister:* For many of us this is a time of sacred memory as we recall the occasion when we ourselves promised to love, honor and cherish. Silently may we once more renew that covenant.

*Congregation:* We rejoice in the grace of forgiveness, the gift of sensitivity and the blessing of understanding. We are glad for the God-given capacity to seek another's welfare above our own; to enter into a union of body, mind and spirit; and to be united in purpose, will and motive.

*Minister:* Love is patient and kind, love bears all things, believes all things, hopes all things, endures all things.

*Congregation:* Marriage is a blending of joy and sorrow, of hopes fulfilled and disappointments borne, of sustaining and being sustained. True marriage is built on love which fulfills another's needs, which adjusts continuingly, which gives instead of demands and which forgives willingly.

*Minister:* As we wish for so much and so greatly rejoice in the privilege of this moment, let us pray together.

*In Unison:* Gracious God, who brings us together in the relationship of love, we pray that Barbara and Bruce will share the joys, the ecstasy, the abiding peace and the rich rewards of marriage. May their love and understanding grow with the years. May they seek each other's happiness, recognize each other's needs and hopes, and each help the other become a person more pleasing to thee. We pray for them and for the realization of the hopes of all who love. *Amen.*

We are gathered together to unite _____ and _____ in marriage, an institution which the state may regulate and the church may sanction; but which can only become real in the lives of two people. This celebration is but the outward sign of an inward union of hearts and as such, marriage is the most tender of all relationships in life.

This couple comes together out of a community of friends and relatives. They ask our support as they together begin the adventure of married life.

We come today to join in marriage Gayle and James. It is our fondest hope that their separate lives may together explore new dimensions of love.

We're here today to witness and to celebrate a marriage. Ron and Mary Jo are bringing the fullness of their hearts as a treasure to share with one another. They bring that particular personality and spirit which is uniquely their own, and out of which will grow the reality of their life together.

Nietzsche says, don't just survive, live! We say, don't just live, celebrate! Cherish each living moment, savor every breath and grow with each experience, so that this attitude will stay with you for all your days.

We are happy that you have come to share in the Eucharistic Feast to celebrate the Christian marriage of Kenny and Joanne and to witness their exchange of vows. May the peace and love of Christ be part of this wedding day, and all the days that follow. *Amen.*

We have come to celebrate Christ in our midst, to share joyfully with Mac and Barbara, to witness God's great love given through Christ and through his body, us, his Church. Let us begin by reminding ourselves that love must be our life, and confess that we have not loved enough.

## WORDS OF WELCOME

*More and more couples are providing their wedding guests with a mimeographed booklet of their own service. Some take advantage of the personalized pages to welcome (or thank) their guests for sharing the joy of the occasion with them.*

Welcome to Our Marriage

Each of you has given something of yourself into our lives. Your love, guidance and encouragement will forever be appreciated. It is fitting then, that you should share today in this celebration of our commitment to God and to each other, to live our lives as one. We are glad that you are with us . . .

Sue and I welcome you to our mountain and we want you to know how much your presence enriches this experience for us.

When two people, Lynne and myself, can be together with their families and friends, it is truly a happy time. Words don't really describe it, but *feeling* is there and I think we all feel it. We're really glad that you all could come. We welcome you. Our hope is that today will be a day when all of us can share the love Lynne and I feel for each other.

We are glad you are with us on this very special day—the day we are marrying each other. You—our families—whose love and laughter, concern and teasing, are the warp and woof of our very lives; You—our neighbors—who have always been there, helping (although sometimes enduring) us as we grew up together on the same block among you; You—our friends from school and work—who are warmth and play, study and career-made-human to us.

*To all of you:* Thank you for being yourselves; thank you for being a real part of our lives; thank you for coming together to celebrate before God our public declaration of love for each other. And please, each and every dear one of you, accept our heart-felt invitation to be as important a part of our tomorrow as you are of our today.

Our love,
Red and Marienne

We welcome you to our wedding because we want to share our joy and love with you.

We welcome you because we need you to share your wisdom and strength with us to help our love grow.

We welcome you because together we can help to make this world a better place to live in—for ourselves and for all future generations.

We welcome you and give thanks for all you have meant to us and for all you will mean to us in the years ahead.

We're glad you're here!

May the God of Abraham, the God of Isaac, the God of Jacob be
with you, and may He fulfill in you His blessing.
May you see your children's children to the third and fourth
generation.
May you afterwards possess everlasting and boundless life:
Through the help of our Lord Jesus Christ,
Who with the Father and the Holy Spirit lives and reigns, God
for ever and ever. *Amen.*


To Our Families, Relatives and Friends
Much thought has gone into our service. We wanted music which would create an atmosphere of seriousness as well as happiness, a meditation which would guide us in further commitment to God as well as to each other, and last but far from least in importance a total service which would bind all who participate into a common spirit.

We have grown up in our respective churches and to us, our marriage in the church is a natural step following our baptism and confirmation. As our families and friends, you have guided us to this point and so we hope you will share the sincere joy we feel today. To some it may recall a memory, to others it may create a dream, but to all we trust it will be a time of renewed dedication in the pursuit of Christian love.

Thank you for all that you have done to make this, our wedding day, a very special day.

> Love,
> Mary and Jim

Our friends, we welcome you to share this day with us. Each of you has given us something of yourself to help us become what we are. It is through your love that we have grown and it is in your love that we have sought consolation. As you have loved us we have loved you and ask you now to pray with us in love to God that the future will be one of peace and harmony for us and for the community of man.

Rejoice with us for this is the day the Lord has made.

We would like to take this opportunity to thank you for witnessing our sacrament of marriage.

> God bless you.

Thank you for sharing this day of joy with us.

> Claudia and Fred

To say thank you to all of you who have helped us in what has transpired here today seems so inadequate. So, to all of you we say, "We love you and may God continue to guide and bless you all!

> Jim and Laura

We wish to thank all of those who have by their presence made this a joyful celebration.

> Pax,
> Jane and Paul

All of you have played a part in our lives up to this point. Today you have shared our wedding. Thank you for being happy with us.

Ellen and Vic

"Thank you" to all of you who have helped us celebrate our wedding—especially our parents, who gave us life; our families, who shared our life; our relatives and friends who helped us grow up to this day.

Mary and John

## WHEN YOU BELIEVE

Words by J. Gibson

*(sung by groom just before wedding party begins down the aisle)*

The setting sun
A pretty flower
A gentle breeze
A summer shower
A mother's love
And someone caring
A singing bird
The joy of sharing

\* This is life you see
made for you and me
It's not too far away
when you believe

The ocean blue
A moonlite night
A tender smile
And candle light
The stars above
An autumn morn
A breath of air
A child is born

Snow on trees
A happy scene
A quiet walk
And grass so green
A garden grows
A grain of sand
A hand out reached to understand


## BIGGEST PART OF ME

Words by J. Gibson
*(sung by groom just before ceremony begins—as his bride
processes down the aisle.)*

There was something in the air
in the haze and mist somewhere
and when I looked around
you're the one that I found
you're the love that I feel
and I know this time it's real
you've opened up my heart
you're the biggest part of me.

For a while I felt so far away
like the sun hiding on a cloudy day
Then you came to me and smiled
and you made my life worthwhile
You're my rainbow and my dream
You're everything to me
For a day it seems such a short time
and I know today that you're mine.
*(repeat 1st verse)*

copyright
James Gibson

# A WORD ABOUT NAMES

Many couples worry about the bride's loss of identity as she gives up her family name for that of her husband. A variety of solutions are now being tried (not without some confusion!)

As a couple plan their wedding, they ought to consider this question because the wedding is a good time to let family and friends know what they plan to do and how this expresses their understanding of the marriage relationship. What are the options?

1. The traditional law in most states is that the wife gives up her family name and assumes her husband's. Thus Margaret Rose Green becomes Mrs. Walter K. Newman or Margaret Rose Newman.

2. A modification of this, not strictly legal unless registered, is for the wife to use her family name along with her husband's, becoming: Margaret Rose Green Newman. Often the maiden middle name is dropped, so she becomes Margaret Green Newman.

3. A further modification is for both the groom and the bride to assume each others family names in hyphenated fashion. Thus he becomes Walter K. Newman-Green and she becomes Margaret Rose Newman-Green.

4. A fourth option is to pick a new name for the new family. This happened recently when a couple were both planning to dedicate their lives to working for peace and decided to take the name of their vocation (just like all the Farmers, Smiths, Cooks, etc.). So they called their new family "Peacemaker" (with good biblical justification). Following this idea, our couple would become Walter and Margaret Peacemaker.

5. It is also possible for the bride to keep her maiden name. This is often done when she has a professional career but can become confusing in legal matters and in the naming of children.

In general, you may call yourself whatever you want to but for legal purposes you should register your choice with the proper authorities.

## MARRIAGE CREDO

*Some couples today choose, before they exchange their marriage vows, to tell their family and friends what their marriage means to them. Couples who do this spend a good deal of time thinking through their commitment to each other, and wording it. Against this background of belief their exchange of vows is all the more meaningful. Some choose to face the wedding guests while explaining their marriage; others face each other.*

We believe in his Providence God brought us together, initiated and nurtured our love for each other and we now ask Him to bless our desire to give ourselves totally to each other forever.

We believe that, though our life-styles have changed somewhat, our mutual love is still a sign of Christ's love and that we are still witnesses of Christ's love for mankind.

We believe that as our love for each other grows and deepens, so will our love for Christ, and mankind which He loved so much.

We believe and hope that God will give us children who will grow in the shadow of our love and through us will come to know and love Christ and all men.

Kathleen and Frank

We take each other today as husband and wife because we feel that our union is the best thing we can do for each other and the good of our fellow man.

Our free decision to join together for life is prompted by the love we have for each other. This love provides us with the determination to be ourselves, the capacity for surrender and the desire for life. It gives us the courage to hope and the ability to dream. Our purpose in joining together is to nurture that love in each other and, as best we can, give it to others.

We now affirm our obligation to work toward the creation of a just social order and the promotion of a more fruitful life for all. We hope that during our life together we shall be able to make contributions toward these ideals.

We also believe in love as the essence of the Supreme Being. We tell you, as witnesses to our union, of our hope to realize that Supreme Being through our love for each other and the world.

We realize that our life in the future shall be both twice as tragic and twice as happy as it was before. But it shall be a million times more joyous. We ask you, as family and friends and as representatives of a greater community of man, to help us realize our love together. And we invite you to share in its fruits.

Jennifer and Doug

## HOW WILL I KNOW YOU?

I will know you by your song
Rather than your voice,
And I will know you by your smile
Rather than your face.
I will look at you and see the strength
I have never seen before,
And I will see the sensitivity that
Will be a partner to that strength.
And I will become encircled in your glow
And thus will we walk together always.

I cannot say
What you will say.
But when you say it
I will know you.
And my response will be such
That there will be no doubt
That this is the sign
We have waited for.
And you will know me,
As the message will rise into the heavens
And permeate the earth around us.

And I will look at you
And not see the shadow
But the substance.
And you will look at me
And see beyond the cover
To the content.
And we will see glorious things

63

That no one else has ever seen before,
But have always been there unnoticed.
And we will see glorious things
That have not been there before,
But will now be there.
Because we will see them
In each other
And make them so.

We will forget
All those who knew us falsely,
All those who knew us partially,
For they did not know us at all.
And we will not focus on one thing,
Giving or not giving approval
On the basis of a part
As others have wrongly done.
But we will see a totality,
The good and the bad,
Accepting it all with joy.
And thus will we say I—Thou
For the first time.

You will know me as I really am
And I will know you truly,
Not even as we know ourselves
And would present ourselves,
But to the very core of our beings.
And we will see the good and bad,
Accepting it all with joy,
And from that time on
Our souls will be locked in harmony.
I will become you,
You will become me,
And we call each other
Love.

—MERYL FISHMAN

The dynamic flow of love is, for us, the heart of marriage. This love emerges from, responds to and is fellowship with God and each other. It is the challenge to create an atmosphere of freedom in which we can both develop our potentials. It is a working together in an attitude of service for common goals. It is a sharing from the depths in the understanding presence of each other. It is a union of persons which respects individuality. It is a covenant of love which accepts weaknesses as well as strengths. It is taking another person completely into consideration. It is the center of trust out of which we respond to others.

Marriage has a consummation in the union of two persons and in bearing and raising children. The joy of this union we confess to be the Will of God. For us to become parents will be not only an expression of our love for each other, but also an opportunity for that love to mature. Marriage is also a striving to understand and experience the meaning of the Church and the home in the context of the fellowship of the Holy Spirit and the community.

We finally see God's love in Christ, which is both redemptive and sacrificial, as the power and the pattern for the way we seek to love each other.


We thank all of you for joining in this celebration of God's gift of Love to us. We do not know what the future holds but we believe our love can help us to meet the changes in life and to grow as persons. We know it is an act of faith to believe in each other without qualification or limit, but we believe that the true realities of life are the faith and love which help persons grow.

We believe we can grow together by working together, not just to help each other, but to try to build a world in which all persons—and especially the little children—can grow in freedom and dignity, justice and peace.

Our love compels us to work together for this kind of a world of new relationships. We will need all the help you and God can give us, but we pledge to each other to give it our best. For us, this is what marriage is all about.


Our love has been like the joining of two sparkling mountain streams to form a greater river. We hope our marriage will become deeper and stronger as the years go by, enriching the valleys through which we pass. We hope we can carry greater cargos and responsibilities as we move through life, joining the great sea of mankind.

We will try to avoid anything that pollutes our lives so our love will remain pure and a source of refreshment for the two of us and for all we meet. Whatever the storms of life, we will strive together to move toward the bright colors of the sunset, knowing that there is always more beyond the horizons of our lives at any given moment.

May our marriage be like a mighty shining river forever flowing toward the sea.

We invite all of you to renew your marriage vows as we take our vows to each other. Marriage to us is a commitment to help each other grow into the personhood we believe God intended for each of us. We pledge to fulfill and treasure each other's manhood or womanhood, joining our minds and bodies in courage when weak, comfort when sad and joy when fulfilled.

We will strive to create a home that will be not only a haven for us and our children but a blessing and benefit to the neighborhood in which we live.

We accept the responsibilities of parenthood and citizenship and will try to live, and train our children to live, as citizens of one world in the family of all mankind.

A RESPONSIVE CREDO, FOR CONGREGATIONAL USE.

Happiness in marriage is not something that just happens. A good marriage must be created. In the art of marriage the little things are the big things...

*It is never being too old to hold hands.*

It is remembering to say "I love you" at least once each day.

*It is never going to sleep angry.* ⌀

It is at no time taking the other for granted; the courtship shouldn't end with the honeymoon, it should continue through all the years.

*It is having a mutual sense of values and common objectives; it is standing together facing the world.*

It is forming a circle of love that gathers in the whole family.

*It is doing things for each other, not in the attitude of duty or sacrifice, but in the spirit of joy.*

It is speaking words of appreciation and demonstrating gratitude in thoughtful ways.

*It is not expecting the husband to wear a halo or the wife to have the wings of an angel. It is not looking for perfection in each other. It is cultivating flexibility, patience, understanding and a sense of humor.*

It is having the capacity to forgive and forget.

*It is giving each other an atmosphere in which each can grow.*

It is finding room for things of the spirit. It is a common search for the good and the beautiful.

*It is establishing a relationship in which the independence is equal, the dependence is mutual and the obligation is reciprocal.*

It is not marrying the right partner, it is being the right partner.

*It is discovering that marriage at its best is described in the words Mark Twain used in a tribute to his wife: "Wherever she was, there was Eden."*

## EXCHANGE OF MARRIAGE VOWS

*At the heart of the wedding—its greatest moment—is the actual exchange of marriage promises. Sometimes the words used are few and simple. Sometimes the original expressions are lengthier, coming also from full hearts.*

67

*Each is highly individual. All are tender, honest, loving, touching.*

*Some couples, although prepared, speak their vows spontaneously, Others read them. If you do this, you might want to place the paper in a prayer book or Bible. That way it is easier to hold and the weight of the book steadies hands.*

I, Charles, take you, Elizabeth, for wife, friend, and lover, and mother of our children. I will be yours in plenty and in want, in sickness and in health, in failure and triumph. Together we will dream, break bread, and lie down; we will stumble but restore each other; we will serve each other and our fellow man. In all things I promise to cherish and respect you, to comfort and encourage you, to care for you and stay with you as long as we shall live.

*I, Elizabeth, take you, Charles, for husband friend, and lover and father of our children. I will be yours in plenty and in want, in sickness and in health, in failure and triumph. Together we will dream, break bread, and lie down; we will stumble but restore each other; we will serve each other and our fellow man. In all things I promise to cherish and respect you, to comfort and encourage you, to care for you and stay with you as long as we shall live.*

I, Gary, take you, Jan, to be my wife, and in doing so, commit my life to you, encompassing all sorrows and joys, all hardships and triumphs, all the experiences of life; a commitment made in love, kept in faith, lived in hope, and eternally made new.

*I, Jan, take you, Gary, to be my husband, and in doing so, commit my life to you, encompassing all sorrows and joys, all hardships and triumphs, all the experiences of life; a commitment made in love, kept in faith, lived in hope, and eternally made new.*

With all my heart, Marjorie, I want you to be my wife. I choose you as the one I need to mature my love of God and my neighbor. I pledge you, Marjorie, to appreciate and participate in your spontaneity, to encourage and support your interests. I covenant to love you in the midst of the everydayness of life: to comfort you in time of sorrow; to participate with you in times of joy; to share with you the responsibility of building a Christian home; to accept your personhood; to allow you to differ with me; to give you the freedom to be creative. I will join with you to seek the meaning and fulfillment of our lives under God.

*I take you, Bain, to be my husband, loving you now and in your growing and becoming. I will love you when we are together and when we are apart; when life is peaceful and when it is in disorder; when I am proud of you and when I am disappointed in you; in times of leisure and in times of work. I will honor your goals and dreams and help you to fulfill them. From the depth of my being, I will seek to be open and honest with you. I say these things believing that God is in the midst of them all.*

I, Ron, pledge to you, Mary Jo, the rest of my life, as your husband, your lover and your friend.

*I, Mary Jo, take you, Ron, to be my husband. I pledge to you the rest of my life as your wife, your lover and your friend.*

*Bride and Groom:* We come here freely and without reservation to give ourselves to each other. We believe that by our love, we bear witness to the union of Christ and his Church. We believe that we are meant to be for each other a sign of the Christ's love. We believe that we are called upon to bring each other to God. We believe that we are called upon to build up the family of God here on earth. We believe that we are meant to give our children in service to God and to mankind.

*Groom (taking bride's hand):* Believing these things, I, Charles, offer myself completely to you, Barbara, to be your husband in marriage and I promise to be true to you in good times and in bad, in sickness and in health. I will love you and honor you all the days of my life.

*Bride:* I accept you as my husband, and, believing as we do, I, Barbara, offer myself completely to you, Charles, to be your wife in marriage and I promise to be true to you in good times

69

and in bad, in sickness and in health. I will love you and
honor you all the days of my life.

*Groom:* I accept you as my wife and call upon the Christian
community to witness our union.

Before the Minister and our present friends, representing as a
small community the society of man, I want to say:

Carol, I wish to be your husband and I wish that you join my
days and my work as my wife. At this moment, I know that my life
as a whole is present in facts and in hopes, conscious and
unconscious. I act with confidence in my past and believe that
long ago this day was prepared. I hope our journey may be long
and every coming day a new deepening encounter.

*With the Minister and our friends as witnesses I happily say:*

*Armin, I wish to be your wife and for you to be my husband. I
approach this moment with a certitude such as I have never known
in any endeavor. Confidently I join my destiny with yours with a
commitment to a task in comparison with which nothing I could
seek for myself is of any value.*

*Out of a firm trust in your love for me, and with an ever-
increasing respect for your goodness:*

*I promise you my love, total and enduring.*

*I promise you my support in the great commitments and the
small.*

*I promise you my own growth that I may become firmer,
simpler, calmer, warmer.*

Nora Clare, I take you to be my wife from this time onward, to join
with you and to share all that is to come, to give and to receive, to
speak and to listen, to inspire and to respond, and in all
circumstances of our life together to be loyal to you with my
whole life and my whole being.

*Michael, I take you for my husband, I promise to be with you in all
that is to come, to love and to respect, to care and to console, to
share the sorrows and the joys, that lie ahead. I promise to be
faithful to you and honest with you: I will share my thoughts and
my life with you and pledge myself and all I am in love.*

In the presence of God and these our friends I, Allen, take thee, Susan, to be my beloved wife. Entreat me not to leave thee, or to return from following after thee. For whither thou goest I will go; and where thou lodgest, I will lodge. Thy people shall be my people, thy history, my history; and thy future, my future. In sickness and in health, in success and in failure, in joy and in sorrow, I trust you to care for our family. And I give you my faith and my love, in God's holy name.

*In the presence of God and these our friends I, Susan, take thee, Allen, to be my beloved husband. Entreat me not to leave thee, or to return from following after thee. For whither thou goest I will go; and where thou lodgest, I will lodge. Thy people shall be my people, thy history, my history; and thy future, my future. In sickness and in health, in success and in failure, in joy and in sorrow, I trust you to care for our family. And I give you my faith and my love, in God's holy name.*

Carol, I hope our marriage will be like the never-ending light from the sun, and radiate warmth even in the shadows of our lives, to accept all children from God with love. May every day of our lives be lived with a full awareness of the existence of each other's love. My heart is open and my soul rejoices this day for we shall become one.

*Giorgio, I entered your life and with you I experienced love and happiness and now I want to become your wife. As the sun is setting, indicating the end of one day and the beginning of another, as this wedding indicates the end of our independent lives and the beginning of a new and joyous life, I will be yours until there is no more.*

I, Giorgio, want you, Carol Jeanne, to be my wife, on sunny days as well as rainy, may we survive through every storm and every season until there is no more life. May the honor that I have for life be the example of the honor that I hold for you as my wife and as a human being.

*I, Carol, wish that when you, Giorgio, look into the joy of our life together, you will see that it is the sorrow which shows us the way to*

71

*joy, and that the two are inseparable. Each comes explaining the other. I have come into your life to share both joy and sorrow with you for ever and ever.*

I, Jane Elizabeth, come forward on this occasion in the presence of God and friends with the intention of expressing my love for you, Paul. I promise to love you all the days of my life—in times of joy, in times of trial, and in times of sorrow. As Christ loved his disciples and they him—so I love you. I love you for what you are to me and for what you are to others. It is my belief that we can better ourselves as individuals and as one by publicly forming this bond. I hope to always be a source of inspiration, consolation, and admiration. Though I love you now so very much I know my love will continue to grow. This is why I love you, this is why I want to be your wife.

*I, Paul, pledge myself to you in a spirit of love, Jane. As Jesus Christ is the essence of Christian love, I pledge to bring the love that is Christ to our marriage. I want to be encouragement and strength to you. In times of unhappiness I want to be the uplifting smile to carry you through to times of happiness. I want our love to grow as I want to continue to learn more about you so we can become closer and truly unite ourselves as one in Christ.*

(*In Hebrew*) Behold thou, Lynne, are wedded to me by this ring according to the laws of Moses and Israel.
(*In English*) Lynne, I will always try to communicate and to share, to feel and to grow. My love for you is total and complete, and I know that it will always stay that way as long as we continue to think and be dynamic as individuals, and to support and care for each other. "I love you."

*Jon, I will always try to share with you, to share my thoughts and my experiences in an honest way. I will always try to keep our love growing and to never let it fall into the trap of stagnant security. I will always try to respect our individuality and also love our oneness.*

I love you, Barbara, and I want you to be my wife.

I want you to love me with all that you have and are. I want you to live with me; to share your thoughts, your desires, your hopes, your fears; to unite your very existence as closely with mine as you can. I want you to see my destiny as your destiny and demand that I be my best, yet to accept and comfort me when I fail. I want you to help me endure and overcome poverty and sickness and selfishness; to stand with me when times are difficult; to know me at my worst and remain totally committed to me regardless. I want you to help me enjoy the warmth and joy of life and of people. I want you to be my lover, my companion and the mother of our children. I want you to be the heart of our home—helping, guiding and adding that which makes life truly worth living.

And I will be your husband.

Together I want us to be a light to the world, a manifestation of the power and the glory of love. A love that begins with us but goes beyond to embrace many others; a love that makes us humble and sensitive, courageous and honest and free. I want us to become, in and through each other, the glory of God that we are meant to become. I want us always to be open to change and growth; to be honest with ourselves and with each other, and then, beyond us, with others; to strive with all that is in us to incarnate the living Truth in our lives and in the lives of those around us; to truly love.

All this and much, much more do I want and hope for; all this do I promise you to the best of my ability. Words cannot really touch the significance of our act here; they attempt description and it is always inadequate. But this, in a sense, is only the beginning—what I mean and want and hope for must finally wait for its expression in my life and in our lives. In all its simplicity, Barbara, and insofar as I can, I am giving you my life—this is what I mean. It is the most and all that I can give you. It is for you to return that life inspired and made perfect by your life and your love.

*I love you, George. Many times during the past year I have spoken those words. With them always has come the responsibility to reveal myself to you with openness and honesty and to create a relationship which would permit us both to grow as individuals and become more loving of others through the knowledge and love of each other. Together we have worked to create the time when "we" is affirmed. Now that time has come my "I love you" takes on a new element, that of total commitment.*

*Not only will I continually be responsible for revealing myself and acting honestly toward you, but I commit all of what has been revealed, all of what I know myself to now, and all of what I will become, solely to you. You will be central in my life and shape its direction in our community and toward God. I will love you, respect you, and grow with you for as long as I live. Through the years other persons will enter my life and affect it, but they will enter it only through the love I commit to you today. They will enter my life through us. I will no longer encounter others simply as Barbara who stands alone. I will encounter them as Barbara-your-wife. We will experience sorrow and pain as well as joy and laughter during our lifetime, but those experiences too will enter our life through our love for each other and be met by us acting together. I am your wife from this day forward. I will walk with you throughout all my tomorrows.*

I, David, give myself to you, Carol, completely as your husband. I accept you as my wife to love and understand, to stay by your side in sickness and in health, at all times, for all the days of my life.

*I, Carol, give myself to you, David, completely as your wife. I accept you as my husband to love and understand, to stay by your side in sickness and in health, at all times, for all the days of my life.*

I, Michael Sullivan, take you, Choeun Kim, to be my wife. I promise to be true to you in sunshine and in rain, through good times and bad, in my talking and my silence, in my waking and sleeping, all the days of my life. I love you.

*I, Choeun Kim, take you, Michael Sullivan, to be my husband. I promise to be true to you in sunshine and in rain, through good times and bad, in my waking and my sleeping, in my talking and my silence. I love you.*

Before the Father, with the Son and in the Spirit we exchange these vows by which You and she and I become one.

## RITE OF MARRIAGE

*Priest:*  My dear friends, you have come together in this church so that the Lord may seal and strengthen your love in the presence of the church's minister and this community. Christ abundantly blesses this love, he has already consecrated you in Baptism and now he enriches and strengthens you by a special sacrament so that you may assume the duties of marriage in mutual and lasting fidelity. And so, in the presence of the Church, I ask you to state your intentions. Laura and Jim, have you come here freely and without reservation to give yourselves to each other in marriage?

*Laura and Jim:*  We have, our love has helped us to understand the real meaning of commitment to God and one another and it is this love which has brought us here today.

*Priest:*  Will you love and honor each other as man and wife for the rest of your lives?

*Laura and Jim:*  We will.

*Priest:*  Since it is your intention to enter into marriage, join your right hands, and declare your consent before God and his church.

*Jim:*  Laura, today we begin a journey which will always be bringing us closer to God and one another. I give my total self to you and ask that you be my wife. I am willing to give and be everything it takes to make us truly happy. But remember no matter what we meet as our lives unfold we will always have our special love for one another. I ask that you accept me as your husband.

*Laura:*   I do.

*Laura:*   Jim, today and forever I offer my unending love to you and ask that you be my husband. Wherever our lives may lead, I will be there by your side to care for you. For my commitment to God and to you will keep us in love for the rest of our lives. Do you accept me as your wife?

*Jim:*   I do.

*Priest:*   You have declared your consent before the church. May the Lord in his goodness strengthen your consent and fill you both with his blessings. What God has joined, humans must not divide.

*All:*   Amen.

*Song:*   "Lady You're My Love" written and sung by: Jim Gibson.

### LADY YOU'RE MY LOVE
Words by J. Gibson

I count the times you've said hello
And all the times you've smiled
Remembering those little things
Which make our life worthwhile
Up so late and sharing dreams
While all the world's asleep
Telling all those secret things
That you and I will keep

(*Chorus*)
*I'll give you laughter when you're sad
and memories for the good times
that we've had
but most of all, I'll give my life to you
Lady you're my love.

I look into your eyes today
And I see yesterday
All the things tomorrow holds
Our Future hopes and ways
A life which any one would love
because it'd be with you
A mirror to your loving heart
and all the things you do.

(to chorus)

I hold your hand for warmth and strength
And find just what I need
A relationship that's really grown
And love was the seed
You're why I feel the way I do
I thank you for it all
But when it comes to how I feel
These words seem very small

(to chorus)

## EXCHANGE OF RINGS

*People need ceremony and symbol to express the inexpressible. Fidelity—the pledged special faithfulness of man and woman to each other—often is signed by the unending circle of a ring. More and more double-ring ceremonies are taking place. When they do, the meaning of the ring exchange has been articulated in these ways:*

*(After reading I John 4:7–18)*

| | |
|---|---|
| Jannie and Dave to each other | Take and wear this ring as a sign of our marriage vows and our faithful love for each other. With this ring I wed you; with my body I worship you; and with all my worldly goods I endow you. |

77

| | |
|---|---|
| Choeun and Michael | Take this ring as a sign of my love. May we be cheerful of face and glad of heart whatever the season. May we be younger than springtime, even to the autumn of our days. |
| Barbara and Howard | Take this ring as a sign of my love and fidelity. Accept my gift of heart and soul as a sign of my eternal love. |
| Armin and Carol | I offer you this ring, a symbol of my enduring love. I ask that you take it and wear it that all may know you are touched by my love. |

*Priest:* These rings shall from this time forth be a symbol of the love here declared and the vows exchanged. Ron, will you place the ring on Mary Jo's finger?

*Ron:* Mary Jo, I give you this ring and place it on your finger as a symbol of our vows which have made us husband and wife.

*Mary Jo:* I accept this ring, as a symbol of our love. I wear it proudly as your wife.

*Priest:* Mary Jo, will you place this ring on Ron's finger?

*Mary Jo:* Ron, I give you this ring and place it on your finger as a symbol of our love and of our vows which have made us husband and wife.

*Ron:* Mary Jo, I accept this ring as a symbol of our love and I wear it proudly as your husband.

*Minister:* Each bring now a symbol of your love for each other. Let these rings say to all that your commitment is deep and everlasting. James, as you place this ring on Gayle's finger, may an infinite love be nurtured through all your years to come. Gayle, as you place this ring on James' finger, may an infinite love be nurtured through all your years to come.

*Priest:* You have declared your consent before those gathered here. May the Lord in His goodness strengthen your consent and fill you both with His blessing. What God has joined men must not divide.

*(Blessing and exchange of rings.)*

*Priest:* Lord bless these rings and may they symbolize eternity and the love with which they were made.

*Groom:* Carol, wear this ring as a sign of my love and the giving that will last the rest of my life.

*Bride:* Giorgio, take this ring as a sign of my love and the giving that will last the rest of my life.

*Minister:* The wedding ring is the outward and visible sign of an inward and spiritual grace, signifying to all the uniting of this man and this woman in holy matrimony.

Let us pray:

Bless, O Lord, the giving of these rings, that they who wear them may abide in peace, and continue in thy favor. *Amen.*

*Groom:* In token and pledge of our constant faith and abiding love, with this ring I thee wed.

*Bride:* May it keep you ever in my heart and mind when we are absent each from the other. *Amen.*

*Bride:* In token and pledge of our constant faith and abiding love, with this ring I thee wed.

*Groom:* May it keep you ever in my heart and mind when we are absent each from the other. *Amen.*

William and Helen     I give you this sign of my love, knowing that love is precious and fragile, yet strong. I give you this sign of our love, an ever-present symbol of the vows we have made here this day. I give you this ring as I give you my love.

Sam and
Susan

This ring without beginning or ending is the symbol of my undying love for you. As it is made of purest metal, I give you my purest love.

Dan
to Marge

Your love is better than life itself,
my lips will recite your praise;
all my life I will bless you,
In your name I will lift up my hands.

Ps. 63:3–5

Marge
to Dan

Wherever you go, I will go:
wherever you live, I will live.
Your people shall be my people,
and your God, my God.
Wherever you die, I will die
and there I will be buried.
May the Lord do so to me
and more also,
if even death should come between us!

Ruth 1:16–18

*Denny:* I am one and you are one,
Together we are one.
I love you, Gwen, and I will be your husband.

(*Gives Gwen the ring.*)

*Gwen:* I am one and you are one,
Together we are one.
I love you, Denny, and I will be your wife.

(*Gives Denny the ring.*)

(*Both drink from the chalice and kiss.*)

*Minister:* These rings are the symbols of the vows here taken; circles of wholeness; perfect in form. These rings mark the beginning of a long journey together filled with wonder, surprises, laughter, tears, celebration, grief and joy. May these rings glow in reflection of the warmth and the lives which flow through the wearers today.

*Bride and Groom place the rings on each other's hand while repeating the following words:*

I give you this sign of my love, knowing that love is precious and fragile, yet strong. I give you this sign of our love, an ever-present symbol of the vows we have made here this day. I give you this ring as I give you my love.

*Bride and Groom, each to the other:*

I give you this ring as I give you my love. As the ring is unbroken, so is my love for you without beginning or ending. As it is made of purest metal, I give you my best. As the circle is perfectly symmetrical, I give you all that I am or ever hope to be. All this I give you as I give you this ring.

## PRAYERS

*There are a number of places during the wedding celebration where highly personalized prayers are appropriate. Bride and groom may join each other in prayer or have the clergyperson pray for them, either after the exchange of rings or at the end of the ceremony, using prayers like these. Other couples will use a kind of litany of prayer during their wedding.*

*Here the bride and groom's own life, their loved ones, the things that are important to them, come into focus by way of special prayer. Sometimes they say the invocations; sometimes someone dear to them; sometimes they find the clergyperson the most appropriate one to articulate their deepest, most prayerful yearnings.*

*In addition to these highly personal prayers, many couples add prayers for the larger society of the church or synagogue; the nation; and for people in need (sick, lonely, oppressed).*

Spirit of the Living God; we thank you for the gift of love, especially the love that brings us together here today. Thank you for the real meaning of marriage in which two become more than they are because of their relationship to each other. Thanks for the privilege we have to be here and to be a part and party to Lynda's and Eli's love for each other and their commitment to each other in marriage.

God, we believe you want love to last and to grow. Help their love, as beautiful as it is today, to become even more beautiful and more deep in the days and months ahead.

God, we believe you have made us, as persons, more beautiful than we know or see. Help Lynda and Eli to find that beauty in each other and each within themselves through their life together.

We know that conflict must come as a part of every human relationship. Help them to deal openly and creatively with their conflicts both by speaking and by listening, by being themselves and by making allowances for each other—in all differences seeking together a better way than is open or apparent to either one alone.

Now we pray for us all that we may help each other learn more about love and the power of love to create, to heal and to build a better world.

Keep alive in Lynda and Eli the memory of this sacred moment. May it be treasured and built up as long as they both shall live.

Thank you, God, for the growing gift of love.

Amen.


O Father, our hearts are filled with great happiness. This is our wedding day. We come before you at the altar of love, pledging our lives and our hearts to one another.

Grant that we may be ever true and loving, living together in such a way as to never bring shame and heartbreak into our marriage. Temper our hearts with kindness and understanding and rid them of all pretense or jealousy.

Help us to be sweetheart, helpmate, friend and guide, and together may we meet the cares and problems of life more bravely. And as time takes away our youthful charm, may we find contentment in the greater joy of rich companionship.

May our home truly be a place of love and harmony where your spirit is ever present.

Bless our wedding day, we pray, and walk beside us, Father, through all our life together. *Amen.*


Father, we know that thou art the Author of Love; that the love which we bear each other is thy gift to us . . . Help us in the years ahead never lightly to regard that gift.

We know that in thy sight marriage will be an eternal union. It is the clasping of our hands, the blending of our lives, the union of our hearts, that we may walk together up the hill of life to meet the dawn, together to meet life's burdens, to discharge its duties, to share its joys and sorrows.

We know that our marriage will stand and endure—not by the wedding ceremony or by any marriage license, but rather by the strength of the love which Thou has given us and by the endurance of our faith in each other and in Thee, the Master of our lives.

We thank Thee that thy blessing will go down the years with us as a light on our way, as a benediction to the home we are about to establish. May that home always be a haven of strength and love to all who enter it, our neighbors and our friends. We thank Thee. *Amen.*


Eternal Father, enable us to have faith in our marriage and make our home a place wherein Your divine presence is felt. Make our home a sanctuary wherein the light of love, peace, contentment, and compassionate understanding are found in abundance— where we worship You through kindness and concern for one another.

May Your law be our guide at all times so that we distinguish between good and evil, right and wrong, justice and injustice, the important and the trivial. Help us joyfully fulfill all our responsibilities to one another, to our fellowman, and to You. May we be patient and forebearing in the face of trials and persistent in the face of difficulties.

Teach us to live each day wisely and well as we share life's journey. *Amen.*

Lord, thank you for the gift of love, especially the love that brings us together here today. Thank you for the meaning of real marriage in which two people become more than they are, because of their relationship to each other. Thanks for the privilege we have to be here and to be a part and party to Nadine's and Bob's love for each other and their commitment to each other in marriage.

Lord, I believe you want love to last and to grow. Help their love, as beautiful as it is, to become even more beautiful and more deep in the days and months and years ahead.

Lord, I believe you have made us each, as persons, more beautiful than we know or see. Help Bob and Nadine to find that beauty in each other and each within themselves through their life together.

I believe that conflict must come as a part of every human relationship. Help them to deal openly and creatively with conflict both by speaking and by listening, by being themselves and by making allowance for each other and by seeking together a better way than is open or evident to either one alone.

Now I pray for us all—that we may learn more about love and the power of love to create, to heal and to build a better world.

Give to Nadine and Bob the gift of memory for this moment. May it be treasured and built on as long as they both shall live. Thank you! *Amen.*

Eternal Father, who art the author of the words, "I Love You," be Thou the witness and the seal to those words spoken here in glad and full commitment between Tom and Brenda.

For the chapters that have gone before this high moment, we thank you—for homes and friends and churches and colleges that have fashioned their lives and shaped their ideals.

For the chapters that are ahead for them, we earnestly pray now. These gifts we ask

- —a steadily deepening love, which grows in understanding and unselfishness;
- —a measure of patience, especially in the early years when life must fall in step with life;
- —the ability to communicate, that they may be saved from hurtful words spoken in anger or grudges nurtured in silence;
- —a sense of humor, that they may laugh at themselves and with others;
- —a happy home, where they may find and give serenity and strength;
- —a sense of values, that they may care for people more than possessions, for honor more than honors, for the dimensions of a home more than the details of a house, for your approval more than the world's approval;
- —a growing faith, that finds your sufficient love and grace in every joy and sorrow and responds in lives of steadiness and service.

We ask thy blessing upon them. In health and sickness, in abundance and in want, in life and in death, abide with them and they with Thee.

## A Litany of Thanksgiving

*(To be led by the Clergyperson, a family member, or guest, with Responses by all.)*

For the vivid beauties of sunrise and sunset,
For the harmonious colors in earth, sky and sea,
For the kindly graciousness of life-giving rain,
For the stalwart comfort of the trees,
For the penetrating and inescapable power of healing sunlight,
For the ministering voices of birds,
For the perfume and harmonies of flowers,
For the cool depths of forests, of caves, and of darkened glens,

For the solemnizing roll of thunder and of surf on the shore, like
   pounding multitudes of hooves,
For the unfailing gifts of soil, and mine, and forest,
For the humbling grandeur of mountains, of stars, and of far-
   stretching plains,
For the laws of the natural world that, through seed-time and
   harvest, day and night, summer and winter, fail not,

*We bring unto Thee, O God of nature, our words of wonder and of
   and of praise.*

For the marvels of the mind, the wonders of the imagination, and
   the untold potentialities of the dedicated reason,
For the gift of speech, the healing touch of laughter, and the
   myriad gifts of everyday friendships,
For the soothing touch of human sympathy.
For the inspiration of martyrs, prophets, saints and heroes,
For those people whom having seen we love, and for the vast
   multitude whom not having seen, because of the touch of the
   all-loving Christ upon us, we also love,

*We bring unto Thee, O God of all mankind, our words of wonder
   and of praise.*

For father and mother love, rooted and grounded in Thee,
For the mystery of a little child, as a symbol that Thou art ever
   renewing Thy race from age to age,
For the desire to find Thee when we sit in our house, and when
   we walk by the way, when we lie down and when we rise up,
For a home where each does his appointed work and "every
   common task seems great and holy" because it is done as
   unto Thee,
For a home whose door is open wide to the stranger,

*We bring unto Thee, O God of homes, our words of wonder and of
   praise.*

For every experience that makes life meaningful: a wedding, the
   birth of a child, the death of a friend, rhythm and harmony,

the pleasures of the dinner table, the wonder and fatigue of
work,

*Thanks be to Thee, O God!*

For the solemn trust of life, for each moment with its opportunity
for joy and for service,
For the deep and abiding love that binds two human hearts
together,
For the widening circle of loving concern that reaches to the
hearts of others while it deepens and refreshes our own love,

*We give Thee thanks, O Lord.*

*The following collection of one-sentence Invocations is indicative
of the wide range of concerns many contemporary couples bring to
the celebration of their own marriage. In each instance, the proper
Congregational Response would be: "Lord, hear our prayer."*

That Eileen and Jack may grow in the understanding and
practice of love all the days of their life, we ask you, Lord.

That Helen and Howard may be preserved in health and given a
long life together, with their family and friends, we ask you,
Lord.

That Peggy and Don may allow their love to spill over to the rest
of humankind so that they may thereby enrich themselves and
all society, we ask you, Lord.

That we may see peace in our days and that Mary and Ralph may
be an instrument of your peace, so that love can grow among all
your people, we ask you, Lord.

That Dick and Maureen may continue to deepen their commitment to each other and to Christ, we ask you, Lord.

That Grace and Frank's hearts may be ever open to the needs of
the poor and the oppressed, we ask you, Lord.

That you bless all relatives and friends of Louise and Mike, all those present, those who cannot be with us, and the faithful departed—especially Mike's father and mother, we ask you, Lord.

That Anne and Dennis shall have true friends to stand by them, both in joy and in sorrow, we ask you, Lord.

That Joanne and Kenny be ready and willing to help and comfort all who come to them in need, we ask you, Lord.

That Chris and Vin have many happy years together, so that they may enjoy the rewards of a good life, we ask you, Lord.

That Sally and Bob's example of service to the needs of mankind may be an inspiration to their family and friends, we ask you, Lord.

That God give all married couples comfort and strength in each other and joy in their children, we ask you, Lord.

That all of us here present will have answered those silent concerns of our heart, we ask you, Lord.

# READINGS

*In addition to the Scriptures, classical and contemporary literature provides many passages whose themes of love and marriage are appropriate for use in the wedding celebration. What follows is but a small sampling.*

Genesis 1:26–28, 31
Genesis 2:18, 21–24
Genesis 24:48–51, 58–67
Tobit 7:9–10, 11–15
Tobit 8:5–7
Isaiah 61:10, 62:5
Jeremiah 31:31–34
Jeremiah 33:10–11
Hosea 2:19–21

Song of Songs (various passages, particularly chapter 2 and 8:6–
  7)
Proverbs 31:10–31
Ruth 1:16–18
Ecclesiasticus 1:1–8; 3:1–10; 26:1–4, 13–16

*Psalms (to be read responsively)*

  29  Ascribe unto the Lord...
  63  O God, Thou art my God...
  95  Come let us sing unto the Lord...
  98  O sing unto the Lord a new song...
  100 Serve the Lord with gladness...

*New Testament Readings*

Matthew 5:1–12, 13–16; 7:21, 24–29; 19:3–6; 22:35–40
Mark 10: 6–9
John 2:1–11; 4:7–18; 15:9–17; 17:21–24
Luke 21:8–19
I Corinthians 6:13–15, 17–20; chapters 12, 13
Ephesians 5:28–33
Romans 8:31–35, 37–39; 12:1–2, 9–18
I John 3:18–24
Revelation 19:1, 5–9

### SONNET XLIII

How do I love thee? Let me count the ways.
I love thee to the depth and breadth and height
My soul can reach, when feeling out of sight
For the ends of Being and ideal Grace.
I love thee to the level of every day's
Most quiet need, by sun and candle-light.
I love thee freely, as men strive for Right;
I love thee purely, as they turn from Praise.
I love thee with the passion put to use
In my old griefs, and with my childhood's faith.
I love thee with a love I seemed to lose
With my lost saints—I love thee with the breath,

Smiles, tears, of all my life!—and, if God choose,
I shall but love thee better after death.
—ELIZABETH BARRETT BROWNING

## LOVE'S SOURCE

The marriage service leaves us looking out along a road that leads on to
endless joy. There will be hardships along that road, and disappointments. To travel it will require strong disciplines and intelligently
worked-out ways. Much that is ahead is uncertain, but some things can
be depended on as absolutely sure. "Faith, hope, and love abide; these
three; but the greatest of these is love."

We can set forth with high hearts because we have faith in each
other which is founded on our faith in God. We can face the future full of
hope because we know what will bring our marriage its daily comforts
and ultimate success. Side by side we can start down across the years
held to each other by a love whose source is in the heart of God.
—GEORGE E. SWEAZEY (adapted)

## OF MARRIAGE

Here Love begins to render the prose of Life into hymns and canticles of
praise, with music that is set by night, to be sung in the day. Here Love's
longing draws back the veil, and illumines the recesses of the heart,
creating a happiness that no other happiness can surpass but that of the
Soul when she embraces God.

Marriage is the union of two divinities that a third might be born on
earth. It is the union of two souls in a strong love for the abolishment of
separateness. It is that higher unity which fuses the separate unities
within the two spirits. It is the golden ring in a chain whose beginning is
a glance, and whose ending is Eternity. It is the pure rain that falls from
an unblemished sky to fructify and bless the fields of divine Nature.

And the first glance from the eyes of the beloved is like a seed sown
in the human heart, and the first kiss of her lips like a flower upon the
branch of the Tree of Life, so the union of two lovers in marriage is like
the first fruit of the first flower of that seed.
—KAHLIL GIBRAN

Love is the seraph, and faith and hope are but the wings by which it
flies.
—HENRY WARD BEECHER

The joys of marriage are the heaven on earth,
Life's paradise, great princess, the soul's quiet,
Sinews of concord, earthly immortality,
Eternity of pleasures...  —JOHN FORD

God, the best maker of all marriages,
    Combine your hearts in one.

—WILLIAM SHAKESPEARE

### JOINED FOR LIFE

What greater thing is there for two human souls than to feel that they are joined for life—to strengthen each other in all labor, to rest on each other in all sorrow, to minister to each other in all pain, to be one with each other in silent, unspeakable memories at the moment of the last parting.

—GEORGE ELIOT

Love is a great thing, yea, a great and thorough good; by itself it makes everything that is heavy light; and it bears evenly all that is uneven.

It carries a burden which is no burden; it will not be kept back by anything low and mean; it desires to be free from all worldly affections, and not to be entangled by any outward prosperity, or by any adversity subdued.

Love feels no burden, thinks nothing of trouble, attempts what is above its strength, pleads no excuse of impossibility.

It is therefore able to undertake all things, and it completes many things, and warrants them to take effect, where he who does not love would faint and lie down.

Though weary, it is not tired; though pressed, it is not straitened; though alarmed, it is not confounded; but as a living flame it forces its way upward, and securely passes through all.

Love is active and sincere; courageous, patient, faithful, prudent, and manly.

—THOMAS À KEMPIS

### LOVE

Joe: I love you, not only for what you are, but for what I am when I am with you. I love you, not only for what you have made of yourself, but for what you are making of me. I love you for the part of me you bring out.

Kathy: I love you for putting your hand into my heart and passing over all the weak things that you cannot help seeing and drawing out into the light all the beautiful radiant things that no one else has looked quite far enough to find.

Joe: I love you for ignoring the possibilities of the fool in me and for laying firm hold on the possibilities for the good in me.

Kathy: I love you for closing your ears to the discord in me by worshipful listening.

Joe: I love you because you are helping me to make of the lumber of my life not a tavern, but a temple, and the words of my everyday, not a reproach but a song.

Kathy: I love you because you have done more than creed could have done to make me happy. You have done it without a touch, without a word, without a sign. You have done it by just being yourself.

Together: Perhaps that is what loving means after all.

—ROY CROFT
(Arranged from the poem)

## EMERGING SYMBOLS

*The wedding is more than the words that are read or spoken. It is a dramatic pageant in which movement and many symbols can be used to communicate the meanings and feelings the couple want to express in their wedding. As you plan your service, you will want to keep in mind some of the newer forms that can give added meaning to your service.*

The *Processional* has traditionally symbolized the movement through life, from childhood to adulthood, usually within the loving care of the family. This is why the father of the bride has escorted her. Some couples today want the groom's parents to escort him to the central place, and to have both the bride's mother and her father escort her. Sometimes a banner, created by the couple, with a motto or symbols indicating their goals for their marriage is carried in the processional.

In another ceremony, the groom, from the pulpit, read the

Song of Songs as the bride walked up the aisle toward him—alone.

The *Giving* is not so much "the transfer of property" as it is the giving of the parental blessing to the couple. When two parents escort the bride or groom, they respond simply "We do" when asked "Who gives this person in marriage?"

Parents may bring the bread and the wine or other symbolic gifts to the altar for the service.

One wedding included a brief statement of the history and traditions of each of the families being joined. At this point the mother of the bride placed her bridal veil on her daughter who was about to be married.

More brides today seem to be making their own wedding gowns—often with their mother and/or friends sewing together.

Some also make a stole—one of the liturgical garments worn by the priest during the ceremony. In this way the couple chooses the religious symbols they find most meaningful for their celebration. Worn by the Church's official witness, there is another dimension given to the unity of their wedding celebration.

One couple not only made a banner to hang from the lectern for their wedding, they so designed it that their rings were attached to it. At the ring exchange time, the best man took them from the banner and presented them to the groom and bride.

The *Vows* are to be said to each other. Instead of facing the clergyperson, the couple face each other and join both their hands. After all, they *are* marrying each other! Some couples memorize their vows and say them without coaching from the clergyperson. Others read statements which are not necessarily identical.

During the exchange of vows, a large "unity candle" may be burning on the bride's side and another at the groom's side. After the exchange, the best man and the maid of honor take the two candles, merge their flames and light a third candle held by the clergyperson. The two separate candles may be extinguished and the newly-lit candle held high to symbolize the new life begun by the couple.

The *Larger Family's* support of the new marriage can be dramatized at the conclusion of the service by having the bride's parents stand beside the groom and the groom's parents stand beside the bride. If grandparents are present they can represent the third generation as they all join hands.

The clergyperson can say appropriate words about the fact that no marriage can live alone. Each needs the support of the larger family. Often the whole congregation is reminded of their obligation to provide a wholesome environment to help the marriage grow. A prayer of blessing can bring this commitment to a climax.

The newly-married couple can make the first act the sharing of the kiss of peace with their family and their friends in the congregation.

After the wedding vows, or at the end of the ceremony, the bride and groom may wish to give their parents some symbolic gift. One young couple brought their mothers a special rose: he to hers; she to his.

At one wedding, guests were each given a flower to remind them of the beauty of life. At another, the guests were asked to bring bells as symbols of joy. The bells were kept tinkling throughout the ceremony. The wedding invitation had read:

Please bring a bell to ring. Come and ring bells.
We're going to celebrate our marriage!

A hippie wedding? Hardly. The bride and groom were both professional marriage counselors. The items used were:

*Flowers* to symbolize the beauty of life.
*Bells* to symbolize the joy and excitement of life.
*Veil* to symbolize the traditions of marriage.
*Fruit* to symbolize all the pleasures of life.
*Food and Drink* to symbolize community and sharing.

In describing this wedding a reporter wrote: "Overridingly,

the wedding celebration was made a fuller experience because it involved every guest. The now-married counselors were particularly pleased by the comment of a female guest who had felt marriage was passé. After the wedding celebration she said, 'Maybe I'll get married after all. It was so much fun.' "

Banners, bells, balloons, flowers, fruit, wine—all can be used in a variety of symbolic ways. One bride baked the bread to be used in the Eucharist. For another wedding the groom created a mobile composed of symbols of life. One couple wore floral wreaths to symbolize victory over the many destructive and dehumanizing forces in life. The possibilities for creating new symbols are endless.

# MUSIC FOR YOUR WEDDING

Compiled by Mary Jo and David Reilly, Liturgists
Kalamazoo, Michigan

## TRADITIONAL

ORGAN

*Bach, J. S.*

"Air in D" (arr. *Whitney*) — G. Schirmer

Aria, "When Thou Art Near"
(Wedding Music for the Organ) — Flammer

"Arioso" — G. Schirmer

"Prelude in D" (arr. *Guilmant*) — Durand

"Prelude in G" (Wedding Music Vol. I) — Concordia

*Boellmann, L.*

"Prière à Notre Dame" (Wedding Music,
Vol. I) — Concordia

*Handel, G.F.*

"Larghetto," (Wedding Music for the Organ) — Flammer

*Karg-Elert, S.*

"Rejoice Greatly O My Soul" (Service Music
for Organ) — J. Fischer

*Liszt, F.*

"Adagio" (Useful Service Music for Organ) — Wood

*Peeters, F.*

"Aria" — Heuwekemeijer (Holland)

*Williams, R. V.*

"Rhosymedre" (Three Preludes) — Stainer & Bell (Galaxy)

*Wright, S.*

Prelude on "Brother James's Air" — Oxford

96

PROCESSIONALS

*Bach, J. S.*

    "Adagio in A Minor" (Wedding Music
Vol. I)           Concordia

    "Sinfonia to Wedding Cantata,"
No. 196 (Porter)       H. W. Gray

*Boellmann, L.*

    "Choral" (Suite Gothique) (Wedding Music
Vol. I)           Concordia

*Campre, A.*

    "Rigaudon" (A Treasury of Shorter Organ
Classics, ed. Biggs)       Mercury

*Ganne, L.*

    "March Nuptiale" (Standard Organ
Pieces)       D. Appleton-Century

*Handel, G. F.*

    "Aria from Concerto Grosso XII"
(Wedding Music Vol. I)       Concordia

    "Aria in F Major" (Wedding Music
Vol. I)           Concordia

    "Processional in G Major"
(Wedding Music Vol. I)       Concordia

*Marcello, B.*

    "Psalm XIX" (Wedding Music Vol. I)     Concordia
    "Psalm XX" (Wedding Music Vol. I)     Concordia

*Pachelbel, Johann*

    "Canon in D Major"
    "Celebrated Canon"       Concordia

*Purcell, H.*

    "Largo in D Major" (Purcell to Handel,
ed. Nevins)       H. W. Gray

    "March in C" (A Second Book of Wedding
Pieces)       Oxford

*Walther, J. G.*

    "Lord Jesus Christ, Be Present Now"
(Wedding Music Vol. II)       Concordia

*Write Your Own Wedding*

RECESSIONALS
*Dunstable, J.*
  "Agincourt Hymn" (Treasury of Early Organ
    Music, ed. Biggs)      Mercury
*Eldridge, G. H.*
  "Fanfare" (Fanfares and Processionals for
    Organ)      Novello
*Goss, J.*
  "Praise, My Soul, the King of Heaven"
    (Wedding Music for the Church Organist
    and Soloist, ed. Lovelace)      Abingdon
*Handel, G. F.*
  "Postlude in G Major" (Wedding Music
    Vol. I)      Concordia
*Jacob, G.*
  "Festal Flourish" (An Album of Praise)      Oxford
*Karg-Elert, S.*
  "Now Thank We All Our God"      Marks
*Purcell, H.*
  "Trumpet Tune in C" (A Second Book
    of Wedding Pieces)      Oxford
  "Trumpet Tune in D Major"
    (Wedding Music Vol. I)      Concordia
  "Trumpet Voluntary in D Major"
    (Wedding Music Vol. I)      Concordia
*Saxton, S. E.*
  "Fanfare and Tuba Tune"      Galaxy
*Wesley, S. S.*
  "Choral Song" (Wedding Music Vol. I)      Concordia

VOCAL MUSIC
*Bach, J. S.*
  "Jesus Shepherd, Be Thou Near Me"      Concordia
  "Jesus, Lead Our Footsteps Ever"
    (Whittaker)      Oxford University Press
  "Like a Shepherd, God Doth Guide Us"      Concordia

| | |
|---|---|
| "Jesu, Joy of Man's Desiring" | Concordia |
| "Trust in the Lord," Cantata 174 (Diack) | Concordia |
| "My Heart Ever Faithful" | G. Schirmer |

*Bach-Dickinson*

| | |
|---|---|
| "God, My Shepherd" | H. W. Gray |

*Bach-Fryxell*

"Praise, My Soul, the King of
    Heaven"          Augustana Book Concern

*Bairstow*

"The King of Love My Shepherd Is"
          Oxford University Press

*Barnby*

"May the Grace of Christ Our Savior"
          The Methodist Hymnal

"O Perfect Love"
"O God Our Help in Ages Past"
"Now Thank We All Our God"

*Biggs*

| | |
|---|---|
| "Lord, Who At Cana's Feast" | The Hymnal 1940 |

*Bitgood, R.*

| | |
|---|---|
| "The Greatest of These Is Love" | H. W. Gray |

*Brahms, J.*

"Though I Speak with the Tongues"
    (Four Serious Songs)        Carl Fischer

*Bunjes, Paul (Ed.)*

| | |
|---|---|
| "Wedding Blessings" (SC 18) | Concordia |
| "Wedding Blessings" (SC 19) | Concordia |

*Burleigh, H. T.*

| | |
|---|---|
| "O Perfect Love" | Theodore Presser |

*Cassler, G. Winston*

| | |
|---|---|
| "Whither Thou Goest" | Augsburg Publishing House |

*Charles, Ernest*

| | |
|---|---|
| "Love Is of God" | G. Schirmer |

*Clokey, Jos.*

| | |
|---|---|
| "O Perfect Love" (Wedding Suite) | J. Fischer & Bro. |
| "Set Me as a Seal upon Thine Heart" (Wedding Suite) | J. Fischer & Bro. |

*Davies, Ivor*
    "May the Grace of Christ, Our Savior"     Novello & Co.
*Diggle, Ronald*
    "A Wedding Prayer"                   G. Schirmer
*Drury*
    "O Thou Whose Favor Hallows"
                The Hymnal of the United Church of Christ
*Dunlap, Fern Glasglow*
    "Wedding Prayer"                 G. Schirmer
*Dvorak, Anton*
    "God Is My Shepherd" (Vol. I)    Associated Music Pub.
    "I Will Sing New Songs of Gladness"
        (Vol. I)                Associated Music Pub.
*Ellers*
    "O Gentle Presence"     The Christian Science Hymnal
*Fetler, David*
    "O Father, All Creating"              Concordia
*Franck, Caesar*
    "O Lord Most Holy"               G. Schirmer
*Fryxell, Regina H.*
    "Psalm 67"                    H. W. Gray
    "Praise to the Lord" (S.A.T.B. or solo)   H. W. Gray
    "O Come, Creator Spirit, Come"
       (S.A.T.B. or solo)        Augustana Book Concern
    "The Lord's Prayer" (S.A.T.B., unison or solo)
                        Augustana Book Concern
*Gore, R.*
    "O Perfect Love"          Augustana Book Concern
*Gounod*
    "Entreat Me Not to Leave Thee"     Oliver Ditson Co.
*Holst*
    "The Heart Worships"        Galaxy Music Corp.
*Hummel*
    "Hallelujah" (Alleluia)               Ricordi
*Jacob*
    "Brother James's Air" (solo or unison,
       arr. *Trew*)          Oxford University Press

*Krebs*
    "O God of Life"
        The Hymnal of the United Church of Christ
*Lang, C. S.*
    "Hail, Gladdening Light" (Evening—Unison)    Novello
*Ley*
    "The Lord's Prayer" (Unison)    Oxford University Press
*Liddle, Samuel*
    "The Lord Is My Shepherd"    Boosey & Hawkes
*Lloyd, Henry*
    "O Christ, Who Once Hast Deigned"    Concordia
*Lovelace, Austin*
    "A Wedding Benediction"    G. Schirmer
    "A Wedding Blessing"    G. Schirmer
    "We Lift Our Hearts to Thee"    Concordia
*MacDermid*
    "Ninety-first Psalm"    Forster
*Markworth, Henry*
    "Oh, Blest the House Whate'er Befall" (Duet)
        Concordia
*Mendelssohn, F.*
    "If With All Your Hearts"    G. Schirmer
    "The Voice That Breathed o'er Eden"    Concordia
*O'Connor—Morris*
    "The Lord Is My Shepherd"    Carl Fischer
*Olivers*
    "Praise to the Living God"    Worship II (GIA)
*Polack, H. A.*
    "The Lord Be With You"    Concordia
    "Wedding Song"    Concordia
*Roberts*
    "If With All Your Hearts"    Theo. Presser
*Rowley, A.*
    "Here at Thine Altar, Lord"
        (S.A.T.B. or solo)    Novello & Co.
*Schuetz, Heinrich*
    "Wedding Song" (high—Lenel)
        (low—Leupold)    Chantry Music Press

*Sowerby, Leo*
   "O Perfect Love"                    H. W. Gray
*Thiman*
   "The God of Love My Shepherd Is"     Novello & Co.
   "Thou Wilt Keep Him in Perfect Peace"    H. W. Gray
*Watts, Wintter*
   "Entreat Me Not to Leave Thee"      G. Schirmer
*Weaver, Powell*
   "Build Thee More Stately Mansions"        Galaxy
*Willan, Healey*
   "O Perfect Love"                    H. W. Gray
   "Eternal Love" (Three Songs of
      Devotion)            C. C. Birchard & Co.
*Vaughan Williams, R.*
   "O How Amiable" (Mixed Voices,
      2 parts, or solo)      Oxford University Press
*Young, Gordon*
   "Entreat Me Not to Leave Thee"         Galaxy

## CONTEMPORARY

PRECEDING THE WEDDING SERVICE—vocal, guitar or keyboard

| | |
|---|---|
| Annie's Song | John Denver, Cherry Lane Music Pub. Co. |
| Anthem | Tom Conry, NALR |
| Beginning Today | Darryl Ducote, NALR |
| Bless, O Lord, These Rings | J. Roff, GIA |
| May Your Love Be Upon Us | Monks of St. Meinrad |
| On Eagle's Wings | Michael Joncas, NALR |
| I Have Loved You | Michael Joncas, NALR |
| Peace Joy and Happiness | Joe Wise PAA/WLP |
| Sabbath Prayer | Jerry Brock & Sheldon Harnick |
| | The Times Square Music Publications Co. |
| | "Fiddler on the Roof" |
| Sacred Trust | Robert Kreutz, GIA |
| Song of the Wounded | Joe Wise, PAA |
| The Wedding at Cana | Westendorf/Kreutz, GIA |

*Music for Your Wedding*

| Wherever You Go | Gregory Norbet, Weston Priory |
| With You I'm Born Again | Connors/Shire |
| | Check Out Music (BMI) |

PROCESSIONALS AND RECESSIONALS—vocal, congregation, choir, cantor, guitar or keyboard

| Beginning Today | Darryl Ducote, NALR |
| Blest Be the Lord (psalm 91) | Dan Schutte, NALR |
| City of God (Isaiah 9:10; 1 John 1) | Dan Schutte, NALR |
| For You Are My God | John Foley, NALR |
| Glory and Praise to Our God | Dan Schutte, NALR |
| If God Is For Us | John Foley, NALR |
| Morning Has Broken | Farjeon GIA |
| Praise You Servants of The Lord | |
| | (ps 112) Robert Hutmacher, GIA |
| Sing A New Song (Ps. 98) | Dan Schutte, NALR |
| Wedding Song (There Is Love) | Paul Stookey |

BETWEEN THE READINGS—vocal, congregation, cantor, guitar or keyboard accompaniment

| All I Ask of You | Gregory Norbet, Weston Priory |
| For Weddings (ps. 102(103) ) | Charles Conley, GIA |
| God Is So Good (ps. 34) | Carey Landry, NALR |

Gelineau Gradual volume 2, GIA, keyboard
   The Earth is Full of the Goodness of the Lord (ps. 32(33) )
   I Will Bless the Lord at All Times (ps. 33(34) )
   The Lord Is Kind and Merciful (ps. 102(103) )
   Happy Are Those Who Do What The Lord Commands
      (ps. 111(112) )
   Happy Are Those Who Fear The Lord (ps. 127(128) )
   The Lord is Compassionate to All His Creatures
      (ps. 144(145) )
   Let All Praise the Name of the Lord (ps. 148)

ICEL Lectionary Music, GIA, keyboard
   I Will Bless the Lord at All Times (ps. 33(34) ) Woolen
   The Lord is Kind and Merciful (ps. 102(103) ) Goemanne

Like Olive Branches (ps. 127 (182) )       Lucien Deiss, WLP
May Your Love Be Upon Us (ps. 32)      Monks of St. Meinrad
On Eagle's Wings (ps. 91)      Michael Joncas, NALR
Psalms for the Church Year,      Haugen/Haas, GIA
    Taste And See (ps. 33 (34) )
    The Lord is Kind and Merciful (ps. 102 (103) )
We Praise You (Ps. 127 (128) )      Ducote/Daigle, NALR
Yahweh      Gregory Norbet, Weston Priory
Yahweh, The Faithful One      Dan Schutte, NALR

AFTER THE EXCHANGE OF RINGS AND/OR CANDLE LIGHTING—vocal
           guitar or keyboard

A Blessing      James Marchionda, WLP
Hosea      Gregory Norbet, Weston Priory
The Lord Is Near      Michael Joncas, NALR
Lord May Their Lives      keyboard J. Robert Carroll, GIA
Praise the Lord My Soul      Tom Parker, GIA
Sacrament      Carey Landry, NALR
Sacred Trust      keyboard Robert Kreutz, GIA
Service      Buddy Ceasar, NALR
A Song of Blessing      Joe Wise, PAA
Take Lord, Receive,      John Foley, NALR
This Is My Command to You      Kevin Mayhew, WLP
Wherever You Go      Gregory Norbet, Weston Priory

OTHER SONGS—vocal, congregation, choir, cantor, guitar or key-
      board

COMMUNION
Dwelling Place      John Foley, NALR
Gift of Finest Wheat      Robert Kreutz
The Greatest Gift      keyboard James Marchionda, WLP
I Am The Bread of Life      Suzanne Toolan, GIA
Love      South American Melody, WLP
One Bread, One Body      John Foley, NALR
Only A Shadow      Carey Landry, NALR
Our Blessing Cup      Michael Joncas, NALR
To Be Your Bread      David Haas, GIA

You Are Our Living Bread      Michael Joncas, NALR
Your Love is Finer than Life      Marty Haugen, GIA


SIGN OF PEACE
Peace Joy and Happiness      Joe Wise PAA/WLP
Peace Prayer      John Foley, NALR
Shalom      Donald Reagan, NALR
Song of the Wounded      Joe Wise, PAA


SONGS TO MARY—vocal, cantor, or choir
Mary's Song      Oosterhuis/Joncas, NALR
Sacred Trust      keyboard Robert Kreutz, GIA
Salutation of the Blessed Virgin
     keyboard Robert Hutmacher, GIA
Hail Mary      Grayson Warren Brown, NALR


Music purchase: contact your local music store or for
Traditional Music: Malecki Music, Inc.
     Grand Rapids, Michigan
     (616) 698-1000
Contemporary Music: Mid-West Religious Center
     Grand Rapids, Michigan
     (616) 456-6660


PUBLISHERS
     Check Out Music (BMI)
     Stone Diamond Music Corp.
     6255 Sunset Blvd.
     Hollywood, CA 90028

     GIA Publications, Inc.
     7404 S. Mason Avenue
     Chicago, IL 60638

     NALR
     North American Liturgy Resources
     10802 N. 23rd Avenue
     Phoenix, AZ 85029

St. Meinrad Archabbey
St. Meinrad, IN 47577

PAA
Pastoral Arts Associates of North America
P.O. Box 110
Old Hickory, TN 37138-0110

Weston Priory Productions
Weston, VT 05161

WLP
World Library Publications, Inc.
3759 Willow Rd.
Schiller Park, IL 60176


(Music compilation edited by Mary Jo and David Reilly, Pastoral Musicians and Liturgists, Kalamazoo, MI).

# THREE TRADITIONAL WEDDING CEREMONIES

## JEWISH*

1. Musical Prelude

2. Processional

3. Bruchim Ha-ba-im...
   "Blessed be you who come in the name of the Lord." (If the ceremony takes place in the Synagogue, add: "We bless you from the house of the Lord.")

4. Mi Adir...
   "May He who is mighty, blessed and great above all, send His abounding blessings to the bridegroom and the bride."

5. If the Maleh Rachamim memorial prayer for a deceased parent of either bride or groom is requested, it is chanted at this point.

6. Address or Prayer

7. The Betrothal Benedictions in Hebrew and English over a cup of wine:

   "Blessed art Thou, O Lord our God, King of the universe, who createst the fruit of the vine.

*Based on the outline found in the Rabbinical Assembly Manual (pp. 27–37) compiled and edited by Rabbi Isadore Signer, published by the Rabbinical Assembly of America, New York, 1952. Used by permission.

"Blessed art Thou, O Lord our God, King of the universe, who has sanctified us with His Commandments, and has commanded us concerning the laws of marriage. . . .

"Blessed art Thou, O Lord, who sanctifies His people Israel by means of this canopy and the marriage ceremony."

(The cup of wine is presented first to the Bridegroom and then to the Bride to sip.)

8 A. The Rabbi may address the Bridegroom:
"Do you _____ take _____ to be your lawful wedded wife, to love, to honor and to cherish?"

The Rabbi may then address the Bride:
"Do you _____ take _____ to be your lawful wedded husband, to love, to honor and to cherish?"

8 B. The Rabbi instructs the Bridegroom:
"Then do you _____ put this ring upon the finger of your bride and say to her:
Ha-rai ott m'kudeshet li b'ta-ba-at zo k'dat Moshe v'yisrael."
(Be thou wedded unto me by this ring according to the Law of Moses and of Israel.)

If two rings are used, the Bride may say:
"This ring is a symbol that thou art my husband in accordance with the Law of Moses and of Israel."

9. The Ketubah (Marriage Contract) is read aloud and then handed to the Bride (see p. 24 for English text of the Ketubah.)

10. The Seven Benedictions are recited in Hebrew and English over the second cup of wine:

"Blessed art Thou, O Lord our God, King of the universe, who createst the fruit of the vine, symbol of joy.
"Blessed art Thou, O Lord our God, King of the universe, who hast created all things to Thy glory.

"Blessed art Thou, O Lord our God, King of the universe, Creator of man.

"Blessed art Thou, O Lord our God, King of the universe, who hast made man in Thine image, after Thy likeness, and hast prepared unto him, out of his very self, a perpetual fabric of life. Blessed art Thou, O Lord, Creator of man.

"Blessed art Thou, O Lord, who makes Zion joyful through these Thy children. O make these loved companions greatly to rejoice, even as of old Thou didst gladden Thy creatures in the garden of Eden. Blesses art Thou, O Lord, who makest bridegroom and bride to rejoice.

"Blessed art Thou, O Lord our God, King of the universe, who hast created joy and gladness, the bridegroom and the bride, mirth and exultation, pleasure and delight, love and brotherhood, peace and fellowship.

"Blessed art Thou, O Lord, who sendest abounding joy to the bridegroom and the bride."

(The cup is again presented to the Bridegroom and the Bride.)

11. The Rabbi then says:

"By virtue of the authority vested in me as a Rabbi in Israel I now pronounce you, _____ , and you _____ , husband and wife, in conformity with the laws of the State of_____ and in accordance with the Laws of Moses and of Israel, and as you bow your heads, I invoke God's blessing upon you."

12. The Benediction

"The Lord bless you, and keep you; the Lord make His face to shine upon you, and be gracious unto you. The Lord lift up His countenance upon you, and give you peace.

"May the Lord implant His spirit within you and grant you length of days, vigor of body, deep and abiding mutual understanding, companionship and love, increasing with the passage of the years and in the fullness of peace. Amen."

13. The Rabbi then continues as a thin small glass (wrapped to prevent splintering) is placed on the floor:
    "At the conclusion of the traditional marriage service it is customary for the groom to break a glass in symbolic recognition of the fact that even in the moment of our supreme personal happiness we are not forgetful of the sorrows that have overtaken the house of Israel in the course of the centuries."
    When the glass is crushed under foot by the groom, all say: "Mazel Tov."

14. Recessional

# ROMAN CATHOLIC*

*Priest:* My dear friends, you have come together in this church so that the Lord may seal and strengthen your love in the presence of the Church's minister and this community. Christ abundantly blesses this love. He has already consecrated you in baptism and now he enriches and strengthens you by a special sacrament so that you may assume the duties of marriage in mutual and lasting fidelity. And so, in the presence of the Church, I ask you to state your intentions. _____ and_____ have you come here freely and without reservation to give yourselves to each other in marriage?

Will you love and honor each other as husband and wife for the rest of your lives?

*Based on the Rite for Celebrating Marriage During Mass, RITE OF MARRIAGE. The English translations of the RITE OF MARRIAGE: © 1969 International Committee on English in the Liturgy, Inc. Used by permission. English translation approved by The National Conference of Catholic Bishops and confirmed by the Apostolic See.

Will you accept children lovingly from God, and bring them up according to the law of Christ and his Church?

*Each answers the questions separately.*

CONSENT

*The Priest invites the couple to declare their consent:*
Since it is your intention to enter into marriage; join your right hands, and declare your consent before God and his Church.

*Couple joins hands*

*Groom:* I, _____ , take you, _____ , to be my wife. I promise to be true to you in good times and in bad, in sickness and in health. I will love you and honor you all the days of my life.

*Bride:* I, _____ , take you, _____ , to be my husband. I promise to be true to you in good times and in bad, in sickness and in health. I will love you and honor you all the days of my life.

*Priest:* You have declared your consent before the Church. May the Lord in his goodness strengthen your consent and fill you both with his blessings.

What God has joined, men must not divide.

*All:* Amen.

BLESSING AND EXCHANGE OF RINGS

*Priest:* May the Lord bless these rings
which you give to each other
as the sign of your love and fidelity.

*All:* Amen.

*Groom:* *(Placing ring on wife's ring finger)* _____ , take this ring as a sign of my love and fidelity. In the name of the Father, and of the Son, and of the Holy Spirit.

*Bride: (Placing ring on husband's ring finger)* _____ ,
take this ring as a sign of my love and fidelity. In the name of
the Father, and of the Son, and of the Holy Spirit.

NUPTIAL BLESSING

*Priest:* My dear friends, let us turn to the Lord and pray that he
will bless with his grace _____ now married in Christ
to _____ and that through the sacrament of the
body and blood of Christ,
He will unite in love the couple he had joined in this holy
bond.

Father, by your power you have made everything out of
nothing.
In the beginning you created the universe
and made mankind in your own likeness.
You gave man the constant help of woman
so that man and woman should no longer be two, but one
flesh,
and you teach us that what you have united
may never be divided.

Look with love upon this woman, your daughter,
now joined to her husband in marriage.
She asks your blessing.
Give her the grace of love and peace.
May she always follow the example of the holy women
whose praises are sung in the scriptures.
May her husband put his trust in her and recognize that she
is his equal and the heir with him to the life of grace.
May he always honor her and love her
as Christ loves his bride, the Church.

Father, keep them always true to your commandments.
Keep them faithful in marriage
and let them be living examples of Christian life.

Give them the strength which comes from the gospel

so that they may be witnesses of Christ to others.
(Bless them with children and help them to be good parents.
May they live to see their children's children.)
And, after a happy old age,
grant them fullness of life with the saints
in the kingdom of heaven.

We ask this through Christ our Lord.

*All:* Amen.

*(The words in parentheses may be omitted whenever circumstances suggest it, for example, if the couple is advanced in years.)*


BLESSING AT THE END OF MASS

*Priest:* God the eternal Father keep you in love with each other,
so that the peace of Christ may stay with you
and be always in your home.

*All:* Amen.

*Priest:* May (your children bless you,)
your friends console you
and all men live in peace with you.

*All:* Amen.

*Priest:* May you always bear witness to the love of God in this world
so that the afflicted and the needy
will find in you generous friends,
and welcome you into the joys of heaven.

*All:* Amen.

*Priest:* And may almighty God bless you all, the Father, and the Son, and the Holy Spirit.

*All:* Amen.

## PROTESTANT*

*At the day and time appointed for Solemnization of Matrimony, the persons to be married shall come into the body of the church, or shall be ready in some proper house, with their friends and neighbors; and standing together, the man on the right hand, and the woman on the left, the Minister shall say:*

Dearly beloved, we are gathered together in the sight of God, and in the face of this company, to join together this Man and this Woman in holy Matrimony; which is an honorable estate, instituted of God, (signifying unto us the mystical union that is betwixt Christ and his Church;) which holy estate Christ adorned and beautified with his presence and first miracle that he wrought in Cana of Galilee, and is commended of St. Paul to be honorable among all men: and therefore is not by any to be entered into unadvisedly or lightly; but reverently, discreetly, advisedly, soberly, and in the fear of God. Into this holy estate these two persons present come now to be joined. If any man can show just cause, why they may not lawfully be joined together, let him now speak, or else hereafter forever hold his peace.

*And also speaking unto the persons who are to be married, he shall say:*

I require and charge you both, as you will answer at the dreadful day of judgment when the secrets of all hearts shall be disclosed, that if either of you know any impediment, why you may not be lawfully joined together in Matrimony, you do now confess it. For be you well assured, that if any persons are joined together otherwise than as God's Word doth allow, their marriage is not lawful.

*The Minister, if he shall have reason to doubt of the lawfulness of the proposed marriage, may demand sufficient surety for his*

---

*While denominational practices vary greatly, the Wedding Service from *The Book of Common Prayer* is perhaps the most widely recognized as representing the Protestant tradition.

*indemnification: but if no impediment shall be alleged, or suspected, the Minister shall say to the man:*

_____ , wilt thou have this Woman to thy wedded wife, to live together after God's ordinance in the holy estate of matrimony? Wilt thou love her, comfort her, honor, and keep her in sickness and in health; and, forsaking all others, keep thee only unto her, so long as you both shall live?

*The man shall answer:*

I will.

*Then shall the Minister say unto the woman:*

_____ , wilt thou have this Man to thy wedded husband, to live together after God's ordinance in the holy estate of Matrimony? Wilt thou love him, comfort him, honor, and keep him in sickness and in health; and, forsaking all others, keep thee only unto him, so long as you both shall live?

*The woman shall answer:*

I will.

*Then shall the Minister say:*

Who giveth this Woman to be married to this Man?

*Then shall they give their troth to each other in this manner. The Minister, receiving the woman at her father's or friend's hands, shall cause the man with his right hand to take the woman by her right hand, and to say after him as followeth:*

I, _____ , take thee, _____ , to my wedded Wife, to have and to hold from this day forward, for better for worse, for richer for poorer, in sickness and in health, to love and to cherish, till death us do part, according to God's holy ordinance; thereto I plight thee my troth.

*Then shall they loose their hands; and the woman with her right hand taking the man by his right hand, shall likewise say after the Minister:*

I, _____ , take thee, _____ , to my wedded Husband, to have and to hold from this day forward, for better for worse, for richer for poorer, in sickness and in health, to love and to cherish, till death us do part, according to God's holy ordinance; and thereto I give thee my troth.

*Then shall they again loose their hands; and the man shall give unto the woman a Ring on this wise: the Minister taking the ring shall deliver it unto the man, to put it upon the fourth finger on the woman's left hand. And the man holding the ring there, and taught by the Minister, shall say:*

With this Ring I thee wed: In the Name of the Father, and of the Son, and of the Holy Ghost. *Amen.*

*And, before delivering the ring to the man, the Minister may say as followeth:*

Bless, O Lord, this Ring, that he who gives it and she who wears it may abide in thy peace, and continue in thy favor, unto their life's end; through Jesus Christ our Lord. *Amen.*

*Then, the man leaving the ring upon the fourth finger of the woman's left hand, the Minister shall say:*

Let us pray.

*Then shall the Minister and the people, still standing, say the Lord's Prayer.*

Our Father, who art in heaven, Hallowed be thy Name. Thy kingdom come. Thy will be done, On earth as it is in heaven. Give us this day our daily bread. And forgive us our trespasses, As we forgive those who trespass against us. And lead us not into temptation, But deliver us from evil. For thine is the kingdom, and the power, and the glory, forever and ever. *Amen.*

*Then shall the Minister add:*

O eternal God, Creator and Preserver of all mankind, Giver of all spiritual grace, the Author of everlasting life; Send thy blessing upon these thy servants, this man and this woman, whom we bless in thy Name; that they, living faithfully together, may surely perform and keep the vow and covenant betwixt them made, (whereof this Ring given and received is a token and pledge,) and may ever remain in perfect love and peace together, and live according to thy laws; through Jesus Christ our Lord. *Amen.*

*The Minister may add one or both of the following prayers.*

O Almighty God, Creator of mankind, who only art the well-spring of life; Bestow upon these thy servants, if it be thy will, the gift and heritage of children; and grant that they may see their children brought up in thy faith and fear, to the honor and glory of thy Name; through Jesus Christ our Lord. *Amen.*

O God, who has so consecrated the state of Matrimony that in it is represented the spiritual marriage and unity betwixt Christ and his Church; Look mercifully upon these thy servants, that they may love, honor, and cherish each other, and so live together in faithfulness and patience, in wisdom and true godliness, that their home may be a haven of blessing and of peace; through the same Jesus Christ our Lord, who liveth and reigneth with thee and the Holy Spirit ever, one God, world without end. *Amen.*

*Then shall the Minister join their right hands together, and say:*

Those whom God hath joined together, let not man put asunder.

*Then shall the Minister speak unto the company.*

Forasmuch as_____ and_____ have consented together in holy wedlock, and have witnessed the same before God and this company, and thereto have given and pledged their troth, each to the other, and have declared the same by giving and receiving a Ring, and by joining hands; I pronounce that they are Man and Wife, In the Name of the Father, and of the Son, and of the Holy Ghost. *Amen.*

*The man and wife kneeling, the Minister shall add this blessing.*

God the Father, God the Son, God the Holy Ghost, bless, preserve, and keep you; the Lord mercifully with his favor look upon you, and fill you with all spiritual benediction and grace; that you may so live together in this life, that in the world to come you may have life everlasting. *Amen.*

# FROM WEDDING TO MARRIAGE

We hope this book has helped you develop your own unique wedding ceremony. But, as we said at the outset, a beautiful wedding is no guarantee of a successful marriage. Instead, it is the lifelong adventure of growing in love that really counts. This adventure requires some real skills, as with two mountain climbers roped together to help each other climb over the dangerous spots. Together they can reach greater heights than either could reach separately.

*We hope you will not become so preoccupied with the preparations for your wedding that you neglect to prepare for your marriage.*

First of all, we suggest that as soon as your commitment becomes definite you consult as early as possible with your spiritual advisor. Allow time for several leisurely conferences with him or her about the nature of the marriage relationship and the adjustments to be made.

Secondly, try to discover in your community those groups devoted to developing marital communication and other skills. Some Catholic Dioceses use a Pre-Marital Inventory, a ten factor instrument which assesses compatibility in such areas as finance, in-laws, communication, interests, children, and marriage readiness. Some also require a weekend commitment of engaged couples in a Marriage Discovery Program. This operates on the assumption that important things of life require preparation to increase chances for a successful marriage and to help prevent some hurting of self or others. This time spent away from the often hectic scene of wedding preparation, allows for marriage preparation. During these days with a team of competent married couples and a priest, the engaged couple is helped to probe the depth of their relationship. They are also helped to attend to the sacramental dimension of their forthcoming marriage, and what they mean in a life of fidelity and growing and maturing in each other's company.

Thirdly, take advantage of the excellent books that are now available to help you and your partner prepare for the inevitable adjustments that must be made in marriage. Of the many good books available, we suggest these as a starter list:

For Catholic couples:

*Marriage Among Christians (A Curious Tradition),* by James Burtchael and others, Ave Maria Press, Notre Dame, 1977.

*Together for Life,* by Joseph M. Champlin, Ave Maria Press, Notre Dame, 1976. A preparation for marriage and for the ceremony, contains scripture readings, etc., plus the New Marriage Rite for Catholics.

For Jewish couples:

*The Extra Dimension (A Jewish View of Marriage),* by Roland B. Gittlesohn, Union of American Hebrew Congregations, New York, 1983.

*Love, Sex and Marriage (A Jewish View),* by Roland B. Gittlesohn, Union of American Hebrew Congregations, New York, 1980.

For Protestant couples:

*Caring Enough to Confront,* by David Augsburger, Penna. Herald Press, Scottsdale, 1980.

*Growing Love in a Christian Marriage,* by Joan and Richard Hunt, Abingdon Press, Nashville, 1981.

*Love and Anger in Marriage,* by David Mace, Zondervan Press, Grand Rapids, 1982.

*Sustaining Intimacy: Christian Faith and Wholeness in Marriage,* by Robert Leslie and Margaret Alter, Abingdon Press, Nashville, 1978.

*The Newlyweds Handbook,* by Yvonne Garrett, Word Books, Waco, 1981.

Our experience indicates that even those couples who have had high-school or college courses in family relations discover that it is different to discuss many of these adjustments with their intended partner. Questions about money, jobs, children, housing or whatever become more specific and require honest and definite answers.

Time spent in developing communication and decision-making skills will help to lay a good foundation for future growth in marriage and will be well worth the effort involved.

# OTHER USEFUL BOOKS

*Wedding Ceremony Idea Book,* by George W. Knight, J. M. Productions, Brentwood, Tenn, 1982.

*Something Borrowed, Something Blue,* by Matilda Nordtvedt and Pearl Steinkuehler, Moody Press, Chicago, Ill., 1981.

*Bride's Book of Ideas,* by Marjorie Palmer, Tyndale House Publications, Wheaton, Ill. 1970.